The 12 Steps to a Community-Led Library

AUDREY BARBAKOFF *and* NOAH LENSTRA

THE
12
STEPS TO A
Community-Led
Library

ALA
Editions

CHICAGO | 2024

AUDREY BARBAKOFF is the CEO of Co/lab Capacity LLC, which provides community-centered consulting for libraries and social good organizations. During more than a decade in public libraries, her work was recognized by *Library Journal* Movers & Shakers, the Urban Libraries Council Top Innovators, and the Freedom to Read Foundation. Dr. Barbakoff holds an MLIS degree from the University of Washington and an EdD degree in organizational change and leadership from the University of Southern California. She is the author of *Adults Just Wanna Have Fun: Programs for Emerging Adults* (ALA Editions, 2016) and the forthcoming picture book *The Schlemiels Save the Moon.*

NOAH LENSTRA is an associate professor of library and information science at the University of North Carolina at Greensboro, where he brings a community organizing approach to the teaching and research of public librarianship. Since 2016, Dr. Lenstra has managed the Let's Move in Libraries initiative, an online space for sharing stories and resources related to public library participation in community health initiatives related to food or physical activity. Dr. Lenstra holds doctoral and master's degrees in library and information science from the University of Illinois at Urbana–Champaign.

© 2024 by Audrey Barbakoff and Noah Lenstra

Extensive effort has gone into ensuring the reliability of the information in this book; however, the publisher makes no warranty, express or implied, with respect to the material contained herein.

ISBN: 978-0-8389-3612-2 (paper)

Library of Congress Cataloging-in-Publication Data
Names: Barbakoff, Audrey, author. | Lenstra, Noah, author.
Title: The 12 steps to a community-led library / Audrey Barbakoff and Noah Lenstra.
Other titles: Twelve steps to a community-led library
Description: Chicago : ALA Editions, 2024. | Includes bibliographical references and
 index. | Summary: "Community-led planning is a method for returning institution-
 al power to communities that have experienced oppression. This book provides a
 unique evidence-based plan, consisting of three phases divided into twelve steps, that
 libraries can use to grow their capacity to engage in community-led work"—Provided
 by publisher.
Identifiers: LCCN 2023027565 | ISBN 9780838936122 (paperback)
Subjects: LCSH: Libraries and community. | Libraries and community—United States—
 Case studies.
Classification: LCC Z716.4 .B267 2023 | DDC 021.20973—dc23/eng20231013
LC record available at https://lccn.loc.gov/2023027565-

Book design by Alejandra Diaz in the Noto Serif, Noto Sans, Omnes and Cabrito typefaces.

♾ This paper meets the requirements of ANSI/NISO Z39.48-1992 (Permanence of Paper).

Printed in the United States of America
28 27 26 25 24   5 4 3 2 1

CONTENTS

INTRODUCTION
The Community Is the
Heart of the Library

The community is the heart of the library. We often hear that phrase the other way around—that the library is the heart of the community. Yet that can only be true when every person feels welcome and included, and sees themselves represented. To approach that lofty ideal, libraries must first center our most impacted and excluded communities, empowering them to build the library— and the world—they want to see. We need to transform our ways of working and thinking, returning power and resources to Black, Indigenous, and People of Color (BIPOC) and all systematically excluded communities. When the community is our heart—when we all are part of one larger body walking toward a more equitable future— libraries can live up to our promise to the world.

If such a transformation feels unattainable or overwhelming, remember that you are not alone. This book is your partner on the journey. Community-led planning offers one method for taking deeply meaningful steps forward. This book will provide concrete, practical actions library workers and leaders can take to shift our organizations, building our capacity to engage in community-led work in ways large and small.

In the first section, you will learn about the foundations of community-led planning—what it means, why it matters, and how to do it. But that understanding is just the beginning. To make community-led work sustainable, we need to transform our organizational cultures and structures to make it our default mode, our normal way of approaching library work. The rest of the book will take you through twelve steps, organized into three phases, to fundamentally shift your organization toward more equitable and community-centered ways of thinking. It will also give you tools to assess your organization's capacity and evaluate your progress.

The twelve-step CoLaB model can be adapted to libraries of any size or budget, serving any type of community. It can be applied as a single large change effort, as individual steps, or anything in between. Leaders, managers, and individual staff all can move the work forward, together or separately. In short, no matter what kind of library you are in or how much support you have around you, there is a way for you to have an impact. Now is the time to put the community at your library's heart.

How This Book Is Organized

Parts II through IV contain the steps of the CoLaB model, describing each one that libraries can take to increase their capacity to share power with systematically excluded communities. Though there is an order to the steps, capacity-building work is iterative rather than linear. You may find that your library is already strong in some areas and weak in others; there may be political reasons to begin at a particular place; or you may find yourself moving back and forth between steps as you go. Ideally, you would read through the steps in order the first time to understand each one in detail and the inter-relationships between them. As you work, though, you can go back to consult individual steps in any order. The steps have a standard format to make it simple to jump between them and find the infor-mation you need. For each step, you will find the following sections:

What It Means. This section describes the step in detail.
Exploring the Evidence. This is a brief summary of Dr. Barbakoff's original research findings that led to the formulation of that step.
Strategies for Success. This section contains practical tips for putting the step into action.
Addressing Pitfalls. Learn about common issues that may arise in implementing this step, and learn how to prevent, mitigate, or address them.
Case Study. This section provides a real-world example of the step in action, from original research conducted by Dr. Lenstra between

2020 and 2022. Case studies span a wide variety of library sizes, locations, and types of communities to help illustrate how these methods can be applied in any context.

Summary. Quickly refresh yourself on the key points from the step.

In addition to individual steps, the chapters in part I support your understanding of the core concepts underpinning community-led planning and your library's individual context. A concluding chapter focuses on evaluating your progress and making adjustments to your process.

Research Underlying the Twelve-Step Model

The purpose of Dr. Barbakoff's research was to increase public librarians' capacity for improving equity, diversity, inclusion, and social justice (EDISJ) in public library planning by exploring innovations in implementing community-led processes and initiatives. For practical purposes, the scope was narrowly focused on public librarians who provide programs for adults. The participants were a purposeful sample of ten librarians, library workers, and library leaders with information-rich cases, maximized for heterogeneity by library size and location. In data analysis, Dr. Barbakoff interrogated the knowledge, motivation, and organizational influences that affected a library's capacity to engage in community-led planning. Four questions guided this study:

1. How are public librarians currently implementing community-led practices with the goal of increasing equity, diversity, and inclusion in public programs?
2. What are the knowledge and motivation influences affecting librarians' capacity for community-led programming practices?
3. What is the interaction between organizational culture and context for public librarians' knowledge and motivation as it relates to increasing EDISJ through community-led programming?

4. What are the recommendations for organizational innovations in the areas of knowledge, motivation, and organizational resources to favorably impact public librarians' capacity to implement community-led practices to increase EDISJ?

The study design used methods and principles adapted from critical participatory action research. The defining value of this research is that practitioners can collectively conduct research on their own work to make their practices more reasonable, sustainable, and just.[1] Study participants joined virtual focus groups followed by reflective journaling on findings.

Research behind the Case Studies

The research undergirding the case studies is informed and shaped by a critical strand in the intellectual history of library and information science (LIS)—namely, that public librarians work differently when they work with communities. An excellent overview of this approach can be found in the 1976 article "Community Development as a Mode of Community Analysis" in which University of Wisconsin–Madison LIS professor (and former public librarian) Margaret E. Monroe examines a national sample of what she calls "community-aware public libraries," concluding that in communities "the versatile librarian may exercise leadership and bring library resources and services to bear in a variety of ways."[2]

In 2020, Dr. Noah Lenstra applied for and received an early career grant from the US Institute of Museum and Library Services (IMLS) to understand how and why versatile librarians in eighteen communities across America work in collaboration with communities to support public health in the form of access to food and physical activities, and related culinary and physical literacies.[3] In total, 129 interviews were conducted, including with sixty-nine library workers (forty-four frontline staff and twenty-five library leaders) and sixty community partners (representing sectors as heterogeneous as hospitals, parks and recreation departments, and community health coalitions). Analysis focused on deeply understanding how and why public library staff became deeply involved in efforts in their communities focused on increasing public health, with the idea being that if we could understand library work around this particular topic, we could understand and support library participation and leadership in a range of community issues, including everything from early childhood development to digital inclusion. This study was also notable for being one of very few that have ever sought to understand how library workers are perceived from the perspective of those community partners with whom they collaborate.[4]

A Note on Terminology

This book will refer to several key ideas for which there are multiple terms in popular use. These terms will be used interchangeably. Although each variation does offer nuance in meaning, in the context of this work, the terms should be considered to have the same meaning that encompasses the broad principles behind them all.

Equity, diversity, inclusion, and social justice (EDISJ). This concept may be found represented throughout the library field as diversity, equity, and inclusion (DEI); equity, diversity, and inclusion (EDI); inclusion, diversity, equity, and accessibility (IDEA); diversity, equity, inclusion, accessibility, and anti-racism (DEIA+AR); equity, diversity, inclusion, and belonging (EDIB); or justice, equity, diversity, and inclusion (JEDI). It is closely related to the concepts of social exclusion, anti-racism, disability justice, and collective liberation.

Community-led planning. Similar concepts and terms from the literature include design thinking, or community-centered, human-centered, or patron-centered design. This idea also is closely related to the Aspen Institute's definition of library-as-platform.[5] It has substantial overlap with asset-based community development, community engagement, participatory design, and co-design. Community-led planning differs from marketing and promotion and is more specific than outreach. It stands in contrast to library-led or traditional planning.

Librarian. The term *librarian* will be used in this book to refer to all library workers who engage in community-led planning. It is inclusive regardless of MLIS degree status or job title. When a point relates specifically to someone with a management or senior leadership role, this will be indicated; otherwise, the term *librarian* includes those with and without supervisory duties.

NOTES

1. Stephen Kemmis, Robin McTaggart, and Rhona Nixon, *The Action Research Planner: Doing Critical Participatory Action Research* (Springer, 2016); David Coghlan and Mary Brydon-Miller, eds., *SAGE Encyclopedia of Action Research*, s.v. "Critical Participatory Action Research," by Stephen Kemmis and Robin McTaggart (SAGE, 2014).
2. Margaret E. Monroe, "Community Development as a Mode of Community Analysis," *Library Trends* 24, no. 3 (1976): 497–514, quotations on 498.
3. University of North Carolina at Greensboro, School of Education, "HEAL (Healthy Eating and Active Living) at the Library," Let's Move in Libraries, n.d., https://letsmovelibraries.org/about-us/heal/.
4. For more information, see Noah Lenstra and Martha McGehee, "How Public Health Partners Perceive Public Librarians in 18 US Communities," *Journal of Library Outreach and Engagement* 2, no. 1 (2022): 66–80.
5. Amy K. Garmer, *Rising to the Challenge: Re-envisioning Public Libraries* (Aspen Institute, 2014).

PART
I

Foundations

This section explores underlying core concepts that are essential for deeply understanding community-led work and contextualizing the twelve steps in this book. Without these foundations, it would be difficult to start or sustain community-led work or build organizational capacity to engage in it. In short—do not skip these chapters! For the more concrete work to make sense later, you will need to develop a community-led mindset through the concepts in this section.

The first three chapters provide a foundational understanding of community-led planning overall. In the first chapter, we explain what community-led planning means, how it differs from traditional library-led planning, and why this approach is both important and effective. Fundamentally, community-led planning means authentically sharing power with systematically excluded communities. Because equity, diversity, inclusion, and social justice (EDISJ) is so central to community-led work, chapter 2 is dedicated to the relationship between the two ideas. Community-led planning is a method for putting EDISJ values into action. Next, chapter 3 adds an applied dimension to understanding community-led planning by describing its steps.

The next two chapters help you begin to consider your own library's capacity for community-led planning. Chapter 4 offers two models of organizational capacity, introduces some of the factors that influence them, and offers an assessment to help you think about where your library's capacity is highest and lowest. Chapter 5 introduces the three phase, twelve-step community-led, capacity-building (CoLaB) model. This model is the basis for the evidence-based strategies that form the rest of the book. By thinking about your own library in the context of the twelve steps at the beginning, you can identify which steps may be most important for your library. Because the CoLaB process is intended to be iterative and nonlinear, you can tailor how you move through this book based on what you learn from chapters 4 and 5 together.

What you discover in this part—both about community-led planning in general and your own library in particular—will be central to how you understand and use the rest of the book. It will shape how you think and communicate about the work you are about to begin. If you think of this book like a guide to growing a garden, in the following five chapters you will be gathering up all the tools you need in your shed. Grab your trowel, and let's dig in.

Community-Led Planning 101
What It Means and Why It Matters

Community-led planning is not simply an alternative technique for developing library services; it is a fundamental reshaping of how power is shared between the library and the community. As such, developing a community-led mindset is even more important than learning the concrete steps. We have to understand why this change is important in order to make sense of how we approach it. For that reason, this chapter focuses on what community-led planning means at a conceptual level, and why it matters, before we delve into methods and examples in later chapters.

What Is Community-Led Planning?

Community-led planning is a method for making decisions that puts power in the hands of the community rather than the library. As a way of thinking about and approaching planning in general, it can be used in a wide variety of contexts. Some common applications include to develop public-facing services or programs; to guide long-term planning such as strategic plans, facilities plans, or collections strategies; or to craft policies, goals, or work plans.

One way to understand community-led planning is through a spectrum of public participation, such as the one from the International

Association for Public Participation (IAP2).[1] The IAP2 Spectrum of Public Participation has five levels. Moving from least to most participatory, they are: inform, consult, involve, collaborate, and empower (see figure 1.1). Do not think of these as a spectrum of worst to best, as there are appropriate times and ways to apply each level. However,

FIGURE 1.1

The IAP2 Spectrum of Public Participation

	Inform	**Consult**	**Involve**	**Collaborate**	**Empower**
Public participation goal	To provide the public with balanced and objective information to assist them in understanding the program, alternatives, and/or solutions.	To obtain public feedback on analysis, alternatives, and/or decisions.	To work directly with the public throughout the process to ensure that public concerns and aspirations are consistently understood and considered.	To partner with the public in each aspect of the decision, including the development of alternatives and the identification of the preferred solution.	To place final decision making in the hands of the public.
Promise to the public	We will keep you informed.	We will keep you informed, listen to and acknowledge concerns and aspirations, and provide feedback on how public input influenced the decision.	We will work with you to ensure that your concerns and aspirations are directly reflected in the alternatives developed, and will provide feedback on how public input influenced the decision.	We will look to you for advice and innovation in formulating solutions and incorporate your advice and recommendations into the decisions to the maximum extent possible.	We will implement what you decide.

Source: Adapted from International Association for Public Participation, *The Spectrum of Public Participation* (n.d.), available at www.iap2.org/page/pillars.

librarians should be aware of which level of participation they are using and whether it aligns with what is needed in a particular situation.

Informing refers to one-way communication, such as a flyer telling people the time and place of a program. *Consulting* and *involving* are ways of asking for input from the community—but, it's important to note, at these levels the library retains all the power to make decisions about what to do with their feedback. An example of this might be offering a public survey to hear people's ideas and preferences, and then having library staff make decisions that take the input into consideration. (In my experience, this is how many public libraries tend to operate now.)

Community-led work lives at the levels of *collaborate* and *empower*—where power is shared equally between the community and the library, or the majority is given over to the community. At this level, decisions are made by or in tandem with the community about important factors, such as what the goals of a project are, what success looks like and how it will be evaluated, what actions will be taken, how resources will be used, and who will participate and in what ways. The community who will use or be impacted by the result play an active role in creating it, with real responsibility, authority, and autonomy. Giving up power does not mean that the library disengages; rather, it remains actively supportive in service of the community's goals.

IAP2 is not the only model that seeks to describe the ways in which an agency may engage or share power with the community.[2] While many other versions currently used in libraries are substantially similar, it is important to note that several models recognize lower levels that cause harm. Ignoring, tokenizing, or marginalizing are performative forms of pseudo-engagement. This is when an institution includes BIPOC and excluded voices only enough to make itself look good, while simultaneously isolating and disempowering the participating individuals to avoid any meaningful disruption or change. Obviously, libraries should avoid doing this.

Dr. Barbakoff has synthesized multiple models together into the CoLaB Framework of Community Power-Sharing, consisting of stages three stages: *performative*, *informative*, and *transformative*.

- *Performative.* At this level, we cause harm by performing participation without authentic inclusion. Because the library is more focused on being perceived as virtuous than on making real change for impacted and excluded people, it ignores, excludes, tokenizes, marginalizes, isolates, or disempowers. This level is negative and should be strictly avoided.
- *Informative.* At this level, we take in or give out important information with an authentic desire to learn and engage; however, we do not share power. The library may push out information, such as flyers about programs or press releases about new strategic or facilities plans. Or it may pull in information, such as by conducting surveys or focus groups. However, the library remains solely responsible for determining the parameters around what information will be shared and by whom. The library also makes all decisions about how to act as a result of what it hears. Asking for input and sharing information are generally positive and helpful actions. However, on the whole, they do not challenge existing systems of power. As such, they have a limited ability to build relationships or take the library in unexpected, highly impactful new directions.
- *Transformative.* At this level, communities and libraries in relationship share power. They strive in collaboration to achieve important community goals. They disrupt inequitable systems of access and opportunity by drawing on library resources to support the goals and amplify the work of marginalized and excluded communities. This is the level of community-led planning. It is a highly creative space that lends itself to entirely new ways of envisioning the library and its services for both library staff and the community.

The concepts of power-sharing described in these participation models are closely linked to asset-based community development (ABCD). In order to be willing to share power with communities, librarians need to see their communities as wellsprings of strength rather than sinkholes of deficit. Therefore, it is helpful to take a moment to understand some of the basics of ABCD. According to the ABCD Institute at DePaul University, the core values of ABCD are:[3]

- Start with gifts. [This means focusing on assets and strengths, not deficits and needs.]
- Build relationships for mutual support.
- Value small.
- Nurture community-led action.
- Work for equity and justice.
- Believe in possibility.
- Lead by stepping back.
- Include everyone.

ABCD and community-led planning are rooted in the idea that everyone brings strengths and gifts, and everyone has agency. The people most impacted by an issue are not helpless victims, but are in fact the ones best positioned to lead the way forward. These philosophies reject the dichotomy between "givers" of social services and "takers" who need them and have nothing to offer. Instead, these approaches treat individuals and communities with the respect they deserve as whole humans, with meaningful knowledge skills and passion to contribute.

Holding asset-based values is fundamental to community-led work. We in libraries must approach our most marginalized communities with the recognition that they have incredible gifts, strengths, and agency. We should be aware that we would be privileged to be allowed to support their work and their goals. If librarians were to come into communities with an attitude of "solving people's problems for them," or imagining that marginalized communities have less to bring to the table than the library, we would be both incorrect and unsuccessful. Community-led work requires us to trust and respect the brilliance of our most systematically oppressed communities.

To summarize, community-led planning is an intentional method for sharing power with communities, especially the most impacted and excluded. Rooted in asset-based community development, it helps libraries and librarians decenter ourselves, our perspectives, and our assumptions so we can truly put community at the heart of our libraries. When communities that have been systematically denied access to authority get to make important decisions about the library's actions and resources, the resulting library services, spaces, programs, policies, and strategies become more equitable and culturally responsive, and they make a larger impact.

Why Is Community-Led Planning Important?

A community-led approach builds capacity across all aspects of the library, from its big-picture values and goals to its daily marketing and operations. We can identify four key areas where community-led planning has the greatest value. Of these, the most crucial and complex is equity, diversity, inclusion, and social justice (EDISJ). Because this takes deep exploration, the relationship between EDISJ and community-led planning will be explored in its own dedicated chapter (chapter 2). The remaining three key factors are explained briefly here.

Relevance and Impact

Libraries and librarians spend a lot of time and energy trying to prove our relevance. We create flyers and web pages with long lists of services and resources. We host handout-covered tables at outreach events and give talks to local leaders and groups. In a social context, we spend parties and dinners answering questions like "Why does anyone even need the library in the age of [Google/Amazon/ChatGPT/insert your favorite new technology or trend here]?" But it does not have to be like this—at least, not all the time.

Community-led planning completely shifts the discourse around library relevance. The library is not out in the community explaining why it is relevant; it is out in the community *being* relevant. The library is there at the table, contributing its resources to coalitions, projects, and initiatives created by members of the community to achieve their own goals. The library is not a separate entity pursuing its own agenda, but a part of the body of the community, a supportive shoulder lifting up the amazing work already taking place. Taking on the role of an engaged participant rather than a solo initiator can lead to wildly creative, culturally relevant, and highly impactful services or directions. The library gets to hear a diverse range of new ideas, serve people in fresh contexts, break out of assumptions about what a library does (including our own), and have a direct impact on community goals. In short, the library does not have to explain to people that its work matters because our communities experience us making a difference within them.

Building Relationships

Community-led programs cannot take place in isolation. By definition, they entail starting and sustaining diverse relationships. Both the process and the result are relationship builders. The deliverables—whether services, spaces, programs, initiatives, plans, policies, or something else—will be useful to, and used by, the communities who helped create them. But an even more effective relationship builder is going through the process of co-designing together, which builds rapport and trust between the library and the community.

The relationships built during community-led planning have benefits throughout the library. Partners may work with us on programs and services, provide input on collections or policies, and promote our events and resources to new audiences. Individuals may increasingly utilize library resources, let us know what they want from the library, and encourage their friends, family, colleagues, and networks to do the same. When a library faces a serious challenge (such as a crucial funding decision, ballot measure, or censorship campaign), our relationships help determine who will stand with the library. Relationships are the lifeblood of community-led work, and they also benefit the library and the community more broadly.

Increasing Capacity and Resources

This factor is what some readers may think of first when considering the value of partnerships. It is an immediately obvious practical benefit. While the other three factors (EDISJ, relevance, and relationships) are more important in the long term, sharing resources enables work to happen effectively in the present.

Working together expands our resources. This may mean money—two or more organizations working together can pool their budgets. Additionally, many libraries have restrictions on what they can pay for due to state law, public or nonprofit status, or internal policy. A partner may be able to allocate a budget for items that the library cannot, and vice versa.

However, while we may think of money first, it is far from the only consideration. Often, a library's most constrained resource is staff time. Working together allows multiple organizations or individuals to divide up tasks or share the load.

Finally, expertise is an important resource to consider. As libraries try to support the wide variety of goals and needs in the community, librarians encounter topics and situations in which they are not experts. For example, libraries may be a hub for people seeking support for mental health, substance abuse, or meeting basic needs; but librarians are generally not trained as social workers. By partnering with others with complementary strengths and subject-matter expertise, librarians can spend their time working from their strengths. Partners who already specialize in a subject can provide deep knowledge quickly. Librarians can support partners' knowledge and skills by leveraging their own areas of expertise, such as providing information and resources, convening connections, and planning projects. In this way, capacity is greatly expanded because everyone involved can focus on what they do best.

Overall, community-led planning is important because it helps align and benefit both the library and the community. For the library, it offers a way to help actualize our EDISJ values, makes our relevance undeniable, builds relationships, and expands our available resources. Partners gain better access to resources, knowledge, and power, resulting in inclusive library services that support equity in our diverse communities.

NOTES

1. See International Association for Public Participation, *The Spectrum of Public Participation* (n.d.), available at www.iap2.org/page/pillars.
2. Other examples include Hart's Ladder of Youth Participation (Roger A. Hart, *Children's Participation: From Tokenism to Citizenship* [UNICEF, 1992], www.unicef-irc.org/publications/pdf/childrens_participation.pdf); the Consultation Spectrum (Dave Muddiman et al., "Open to All? The Public Library and Social Exclusion: Executive Summary," *New Library World* 102, no. 4/5 [2001]: 154–58); Edmonton Public Library's Levels of Community Engagement (Edmonton Public Library, *EPL Community-Led Toolkit* [2016], https://epl.bibliocms.com/wp-content/uploads/sites/18/2015/08/EPL-Community-Led-Toolkit-Final-EXTERNAL-Web.pdf.); the Public Involvement Continuum (John Pateman and Ken Williment, *Developing Community-Led Public Libraries: Evidence from the UK and Canada* [Ashgate Publishing, 2013]; Working Together Project, *Community-Led Libraries Toolkit* [2008], www.vpl.ca/sites/default/files/Community-Led-Libraries-Toolkit.pdf); Strive Together Co-development of Solutions (2020); and the Spectrum of Community Engagement to Ownership from Facilitating Power (Rosa González, *The Spectrum of Community Engagement to Ownership: Facilitating Power* [Facilitating Power, 2020], www.facilitatingpower.com/spectrum_of_community_engagement_to_ownership).
3. Asset-Based Community Development Institute, "Values behind ABCD," DePaul University, n.d., https://resources.depaul.edu/abcd-institute/about/Pages/Values.aspx.

Relationship to Equity, Diversity, Inclusion, and Social Justice

As referenced in the previous chapter, EDISJ is the primary reason to engage in community-led planning. This topic is extensive and important enough to merit its own chapter. The systems of inequity that community-led planning are intended to address have deep roots in the profession as well as society at large. To conduct community-led planning effectively, it is essential to understand why and how it is intended to lead to more equitable libraries and communities, and how it interacts with existing systems of power.

Community-led planning is a way to put our EDISJ values into action.[1] EDISJ is a core value of the library profession, as affirmed by major library organizations such as the American Library Association, Public Library Association, and International Federation of Library Associations.[2] Though the terms used may be different, EDISJ is also likely part of your own library's values, mission, vision, or strategy. If you have a statement addressing the idea that your library strives to be open, welcoming, or accessible to all, then you hold an EDISJ-related value.

But how do we go beyond words and statements? What actions can libraries and librarians actually take to dismantle oppressive systems and help build more equitable communities? Community-led planning can be part of the answer. When a library engages in a community-led process, it returns power to the community. It is the community, not the library, who decides what the goals of the project will be and what success looks like. It is the community, not the library, who decides what actions need to be taken. The library puts real resources—like space, staff time, information, and expertise in research and project management—at the disposal of the community in the service of accomplishing their aspirations. In short, community-led planning builds equity by putting the library's institutional power and resources back into the hands of communities who have been systematically denied these things.

Librarians must understand, however, that even in a process designed purposefully to enhance equity, an equitable result is not a given. Librarians must choose to intentionally center the voices of the most impacted and systematically excluded. It would be easy for a library to go through the steps of a community-led process with the same established partners and patrons we already serve well. The process would likely be comfortable and enjoyable, and the resulting service or product good. But the process would not transform systems; the result would not transfer power back to marginalized communities. To engage in fundamentally transformative equity work, librarians must consistently ask who is impacted and systematically excluded, and actively center those communities.

The importance of employing all methods possible to increase equity, including community-led planning, cannot be overstated. BIPOC and other marginalized communities deserve better library service. Despite the library profession's intent to be open to all, marginalized and underserved communities do not experience library services equitably. Many populations experience barriers to full library use,[3] including BIPOC communities, racial and ethnic minorities, people with disabilities, immigrants and refugees, older adults, people experiencing mental illness, neurodivergent people, people experiencing homelessness, the LGBTQIA+ community, justice-involved and decarcerated people, and others.

These disparities are partially rooted in and exacerbated by the persistent exclusion of BIPOC and other marginalized people from the library profession. The field struggles profoundly with recruiting, retaining, and allowing the full participation of BIPOC librarians and those holding other marginalized identities—even as the communities that libraries serve are becoming more diverse. Data demonstrate that the demographic makeup of librarianship has persistently lagged behind the population at large and has not improved significantly since the civil rights era.[4] The dire state of diversity in the profession prompted an ALA report on librarian demographics to conclude,

> If libraries are to remain relevant they must be willing to not only reach out to diverse communities but to build a workforce reflective of that diversity. This effort will not be an act of altruism, but of survival.[5]

While this book's focus on community-led planning does not explicitly address the makeup of the profession, the two are interrelated. Systemic inequity and systems of oppression that exclude BIPOC and people holding other marginalized identities harm both librarians and communities. The underrepresentation of these important voices and lived experiences makes both our external services and our internal cultures less welcoming and just. We must continue to work to make librarianship more inclusive for BIPOC staff and those holding marginalized identities. We must also, simultaneously, strive to make our services more reflective of the people we serve. Ideally, as we do one, we will also indirectly support the other.[6] When we engage in systems change to disrupt hegemonic power structures in libraries—such as by adopting community-led practices and by taking steps to make the profession more inclusive—we are striving for a more equitable environment where a diverse community of both staff and patrons can thrive.

The traditional ways libraries think about, plan for, and provide equal rather than equitable access result directly in practices that actively exclude minoritized communities and reinforce hegemonic values. In the seminal study "Open to All? The Public Library and Social Exclusion," the authors conducted eighteen months of research that included a survey of all UK public library districts.[7] They found that only one-sixth of all public libraries adhered to best practices for social inclusion.

The authors concluded that public libraries' primarily White, middle-class staff tended toward passive, "weak, voluntary and 'take it or leave it' approaches to social inclusion." It is important to note that the authors attributed this not to a *failure* of the library's commitment to access, but to one of its defining *features*. They wrote, "The core rationale of the public library movement continues to be based on the idea of developing universal access to a service which essentially reflects mainstream middle-class, white and English values."[8]

This rationale has resulted in multiple organizational, cultural, and environmental barriers to library use, effectively excluding many marginalized groups and low-income people. People who say they have never been to a public library in their lives are more likely than the general population to be Black, Hispanic, over the age of 65, or low income, or to hold a high school diploma or less.[9] In interviews with the Working Together Project, patrons from socially excluded groups described limiting or stopping their library use due to experiences such as fear of visiting the library due to a misunderstanding of fines structures and enforcement, embarrassment over accidentally violating unspoken cultural norms, and difficulty navigating physical spaces.[10]

This is not to imply that socially excluded groups do not use libraries at all or that they have solely negative perceptions of libraries. Rather, it suggests that usage numbers alone do not tell the full story because minoritized patrons may be provided with qualitatively poorer library experiences even when the quantity of their usage is similar.[11] Libraries remain an essential lifeline for many people of all backgrounds, and library resources may be especially important for people with low incomes or in communities that are systematically denied other resources. In a study of the role of social infrastructure in community resilience, Eric Klinenberg found that neighborhoods with robust community gathering spaces, including libraries, were vastly safer and healthier than demographically similar neighborhoods without them.[12] That many people from marginalized communities continue to use and love libraries despite encountering multiple barriers only reinforces the importance of making libraries more equitable.

Given the structural nature of EDISJ issues in librarianship as a profession and library service to the public, it is reasonable to wonder if structural changes to the way libraries design and implement public services, programs, and spaces might mitigate some of the biases and harms in existing models. Research does indeed demonstrate that an entirely different planning structure—one built on sharing power with communities rather than concentrating it in the hands of librarians, and on active inclusion rather than passive access—can be employed to increase EDISJ in public services, even when other barriers are present.[13]

In short, people of all backgrounds report using and valuing libraries, but libraries are not serving all people equitably. Patterns of oppression and exclusion in library services mirror those operating in society at large.[14] Libraries are systematically more effective at engaging people, both in numbers and in quality, who already have privilege and resources.[15] This is the problem community-led planning can help to solve.

NOTES

1. See Audrey Barbakoff, "Building Capacity for Equity, Diversity, and Inclusion in Public Library Programs through Community-Led Practices: An Innovation Model" (PhD diss., University of Southern California, 2021).

2. See American Library Association, *American Library Association Strategic Directions* (2017), www.ala.org/aboutala/sites/ala.org.aboutala/files/content/governance/StrategicPlan/Strategic%20Directions%202017_Update.pdf; American Library Association, *Equity, Diversity, Inclusion: An Interpretation of the Library Bill of Rights* (2017), www.ala.org/advocacy/intfreedom/librarybill/interpretations/EDI; Christie Koontz and Barbara Gubbin, *IFLA Public Library Service Guidelines* (De Gruyter Saur, 2010), https://doi.org/10.1515/9783110232271; and L. L. Thompson and C. Fuller-Gregory, *The Movement toward Equity*, Public Libraries (2020), http://publiclibrariesonline.org/2020/05/the-movement-toward-equity/.

3. Nicole A. Cooke, *Information Services to Diverse Population: Developing Culturally Competent Library Professionals* (Libraries Unlimited, 2017).

4. American Library Association, *Diversity Counts!* (2007), www.ala.org/aboutala/sites/ ala.org.aboutala/files/content/diversity/diversitycounts/diversitycounts_rev0.pdf; Nicole A. Cooke, "The Spectrum Doctoral

Fellowship Program: Enhancing the LIS Professoriate," *InterActions: UCLA Journal of Education and Information Studies* 10, no. 1 (2014); Paul Jaeger and Renee Franklin, "The Virtuous Circle: Increasing Diversity in LIS Faculties to Create More Inclusive Library Services and Outreach," *Education Libraries* 30, no. 1 (2007): 20–26, https://doi.org/10.26443/el.v30i1.233; Kyung-Sun Kim and Sei-Ching Joanna Sin, "Recruiting and Retaining Students of Color in LIS Programs: Perspectives of Library and Information Professionals," *Journal of Education for Library and Information Science* 47, no. 2 (2006): 81–95, https://doi.org/10.2307/40324324; Herman L. Totten, "Ethnic Diversity in Library Schools: Completing the Education Cycle," *Texas Library Journal* 76, no. 1 (2000): 16–19; Jennifer Vinopal, "The Quest for Diversity in Library Staffing: From Awareness to Action," In the Library with the Lead Pipe, 2015, www.inthelibrarywiththeleadpipe.org/2016/quest-for-diversity/.

5. American Library Association, *Diversity Counts!*, 4.
6. Jaeger and Franklin, "The Virtuous Circle."
7. Dave Muddiman et al., "Open to All? The Public Library and Social Exclusion: Executive Summary," *New Library World* 102, no. 4/5 (2001): 154–58, https://doi.org/10.1108/03074800110390626.
8. Dave Muddiman et al., "Open to All? The Public Library and Social Exclusion: Volume One Overview and Conclusions," *Library and Information Commission Report* 84 (2000): viii.
9. John B. Horrigan, "Libraries 2016," Pew Research Center, September 9, 2016, www.pewinternet.org/2016/09/09/2016/Libraries-2016/.
10. Working Together Project, *Community-Led Libraries Toolkit* (2008), www.vpl.ca/sites/default/files/Community-Led-Libraries-Toolkit.pdf.
11. Amy Sonnie, *Advancing Racial Equity in Public Libraries: Case Studies from the Field* (Government Alliance on Race and Equity, 2018), www.racialequityalliance.org/wp-content/uploads/2018/04/GARE_Libraries Report_v8_DigitalScroll_WithHyperlinks.pdf.
12. Eric Klinenberg, *Palaces for the People: How Social Infrastructure Can Help Fight Inequality, Polarization, and the Decline of Civic Life* (Crown, 2018).

13. Muddiman et al., "Open to All?"; John Pateman and Ken Williment, *Developing Community-Led Public Libraries: Evidence from the UK and Canada* (Ashgate Publishing, 2013); Working Together Project, *Community-Led Libraries Toolkit.*
14. Horrigan, "Libraries 2016"; Klinenberg, *Palaces for the People*; Pew Research Center, "From Distant Admirers to Library Lovers: A Typology of Public Library Engagement in America," April 13, 2014, http://libraries.pewinternet.org/2014/03/13/typology/.
15. Muddiman et al., "Open to All?"; Pew Research Center, "From Distant Admirers to Library Lovers."

How to Conduct
Community-Led Planning

D id you jump straight to this chapter before reading the previous ones? When Dr. Barbakoff talked with librarians about community-led planning, one of the most frequent comments she heard is that they just do not know how to do it. If they knew the steps, they reason, they could start using community-led methods right away. But her research painted a very different picture of what people really need. Learning the "how" is actually one of the least important actions you can take (making this chapter the least important one in the book!).

Procedural knowledge alone simply is not enough to launch and sustain community-led work. The steps of community-led methods have been widely published and easily available for more than two decades, yet access to this information has not translated into widespread adoption. Conversely, Dr. Barbakoff has seen over and over that librarians who start with no idea of how to proceed can still dive in, figure things out as they go, and have wild successes.

A step-by-step process is of limited use because every community-led project unfolds in a unique way. Each is a combination of a specific community at a particular moment in time working on a different project. The library cannot and should not try to impose a rigid set of steps and schedule because the community determines how the process will unfold. Libraries must be flexible and grounded enough to adapt to the changing circumstances, and committed enough to dive in and persist despite ambiguity, all without losing sight of their true goals and principles. To accomplish this, feeling and understanding the importance and purpose of community-led work is much more important than learning the steps, even if it does not seem so at first. That is why we encourage you not to skip the first chapters in this book, even if that means going backward after a peek at this one. Along with the rest of this book, they will help you develop the mindset and the individual and organizational capacity that bring these steps to life.

One of the clearest models for how to conduct community-led planning in libraries comes from the Working Together Project, an initiative of four Canadian libraries that ran from 2004 to 2008. Over those four years, Halifax Public Libraries, Regina Public Library, Toronto Public Library, and Vancouver Public Library experimented with a variety of community development techniques to establish relationships with, and reduce systemic barriers for, excluded and marginalized populations. They distilled their successful methods into the *Community-Led Libraries Toolkit*, published in 2008. While others have built on their work, such as Edmonton Public Library's toolkit with more operational details released a few years later, the core of the model remains effective and relevant.[1] Here, we have adapted the language somewhat to emphasize a focus on community strengths and assets rather than deficits and needs. The stages in a community-led process are:

1. Systematically build knowledge about community (community assessment).
2. Identify community goals and needs.
3. Plan services.
4. Deliver services.
5. Evaluate results.

The broad stages themselves are similar to traditional library-led planning, where library staff determine how a process will develop and control what the final actions or products will be. However, the *way* each stage unfolds is very different. Figure 3.1 is based on the Working Together Project's *Community-Led Libraries Toolkit.* It

FIGURE 3.1

Community-Led Service Planning: Key Differences

	Community assessment & needs identification		Service planning & delivery		Evaluation
	Community assessment	Needs identification	Service planning	Delivery	

TRADITIONAL PLANNING	Staff review:
	• demograph-
	  ic data
	• library use
	  statistics
	• comment
	  cards
	• community
	  survey
	  results
		Staff identify service gaps or underserved communities.	• Staff review
			  literature.
			• Staff consult
			  with other
			  staff and
			  service
			  providers.
			• Staff devel-
			  op service
			  response.
				Staff deliver service:
				• develop the
				  collection
				• hold the
				  program
				• design
				  facilities
					Staff review various inputs, such as:
					• feedback
					  forms
					• program
					  attendance
					• collection
					  use
					• library card
					  enrollment
					• other
					  statistics

COMMUNITY-LED PLANNING	Staff review all of the above
	• Staff spend
	  time in the
	  community
	  developing
	  relation-
	  ships with
	  community
	  members.
	• Staff hear
	  from the
	  community
	  about what
	  is important
	  to them.
		Staff discuss with commu-nity members and hear from the community what their priorities are.	• Service
			  ideas are the
			  community's
			  ideas.
			• Community
			  is engaged
			  in the plan-
			  ning of the
			  service.
			• Staff act as
			  partners and
			  facilitators
			  rather than
			  creators and
			  teachers.
				• Community
				  members
				  and staff
				  work togeth-
				  er to deliver
				  the service.
				• Community
				  members
				  are involved
				  in selecting
				  collection
				  materials.
				• Community
				  members
				  are active in
				  hosting the
				  program.
				• Community
				  members
				  work col-
				  laboratively
				  with the
				  library to de-
				  velop policy
				  recommen-
				  dations.
					Staff review various inputs:
					• all of the
					  above
					
					And commu-nity and staff discuss:
					• How did
					  the process
					  work?
					• Did the ser-
					  vice/policy,
					  etc., actually
					  address the
					  need?
					• What could
					  have been
					  done differ-
					  ently?

Source: Adapted from Working Together Project, *Community-Led Libraries Toolkit* (2008), www.vpl.ca/sites/default/files/Community-Led-Libraries-Toolkit.pdf.

provides a brief side-by-side comparison of how each stage of planning differs between library-led and community-led planning methods.

Let's take a closer look at some of the differences described in the figure. In traditional planning, libraries treat community assessment and identifying community priorities as a largely internal, point-in-time process. For example, as part of a scheduled strategic planning process, a librarian might look at school district or census statistics to see which populations or languages are growing. If libraries solicit input, it is often in the form of a survey—informational rather than participatory and part of a formal, time-bound process. In community-led planning, understanding the community and its priorities comes from building ongoing relationships with minoritized communities. Librarians consistently embed in the community, such as by joining BIPOC-led coalitions and organizations, contributing to community and cultural celebrations, or simply spending time as part of the community in spaces created by the community for itself. Drawing on their sustained relationships of mutual trust and respect, librarians invite dialogue with other community members and leaders about their priorities and aspirations. (This is not to say that community-led planning ignores statistics and data; it simply sees them as incomplete on their own, one small piece of the puzzle. More on this in step 9.)

Another key difference appears in service planning and delivery. In traditional library-led planning, the library makes all the decisions and manages the execution. Staff generate their own service ideas from professional and community news; by requesting specific input from colleagues or service providers; or perhaps from comments left by patrons who are already library users. Then staff plan the programs, write the policies, make the booklists, choose the furniture, or set the strategic goals, etc. In a community-led model, the community generates the ideas. Individuals and groups from that community are also directly involved in planning and delivering the service. They have real responsibility, authority to make autonomous decisions, and accountability for the outcomes. Librarians serve as conveners and facilitators, providing access to library resources and support. Because the people who will use the service or be impacted by the decision are the ones who plan and implement it, the result is deeply rooted in the community's own priorities, cultures, experiences, and strengths.

A community-led perspective also reshapes evaluation. Traditional library-led planning relies heavily on standard output statistics like attendance, circulation, or door count, and at times on one-way patron feedback such as surveys or comment cards. It tends to take place at the conclusion of a program, pilot, or project. In a community-led model, the library facilitates conversations with the community to identify what success means to them and to determine how to evaluate progress toward that goal. The community's definition of success may be highly qualitative, may focus more on impact than on attendance, and may require new ways of gathering and interpreting knowledge.

Ideally, these evaluation conversations would happen at the beginning of a process, before any specific actions are planned. This is because understanding what the community truly wants from a project is essential to being able to create a result that achieves it. (Starting by envisioning an end point and then working backward to determine actions is often called outcome-based planning and evaluation. The concise book *Five Steps of Outcome-Based Planning and Evaluation for Public Libraries* provides an excellent starting point for learning this method.[2]) Developing a clear, shared vision of what success looks like early on prevents missteps based on inaccurate assumptions.

There are other models besides the Working Together Project that provide step-by-step or detailed practical information on how to engage in community-led planning. They generally draw on the same pool of underlying principles; however, each offers nuances and tools that may provide additional insight. For example, the design firm IDEO produced a 2015 guide on *Design Thinking for Libraries*, which offers strategies for engaging community in participatory design. The Aspen Institute's 2014 report *Rising to the Challenge: Re-envisioning Public Libraries* explores the idea of the library as a platform for community to pursue its goals. The Government Alliance on Race and Equity (GARE) published *Advancing Racial Equity in Libraries* in 2018. The report divides up phases differently (normalize, organize, and operationalize) and includes the use of racial-equity assessments to understand impact, maximize benefits, and minimize harms. Edmonton Public Library's *Community-Led Toolkit* applies many of the same principles and processes found in the Working Together Project to a specific library system, but includes more practical details, such as lists of how staff in different positions engaged with the work, an example of a completed community profile, and an evaluation checklist.[3]

Overall, a community-led process follows similar steps to a traditional library-led one, moving from assessment to planning to delivery to evaluation. The true differences lie in the way these steps take place—through sustained relationships, dialogue, and shared action with the most impacted communities. While library-led programs follow the steps in a mostly linear fashion, community-led planning addresses them iteratively or cyclically. We continually revisit each step to keep all parties in alignment, and we often engage in multiple or overlapping projects that build on each other over time.

Community-led planning values the process and the relationships it builds as much as it values the product. It treats human relationships as a valid way of knowing and doing. Because this work is relational, process oriented, and cross-cultural, every community-led effort is unique. The timeline, the communication strategies, what tasks take place, and who is responsible for them—these all will vary. What stays constant is our understanding of why we are doing this work and a commitment to contributing to a more equitable community. The twelve steps in this book are designed to help you transform the culture, systems, and mindsets of your library to build and sustain your capacity to be led by your community.

NOTES

1. See Edmonton Public Library, *EPL Community-Led Toolkit* (2016), https://epl.bibliocms.com/wp-content/uploads/sites/18/2015/08/EPL-Community-Led-Toolkit-Final-EXTERNAL-Web.pdf.
2. See Melissa Gross, Cindy Mediavilla, and Virginia A. Walter, *Five Steps of Outcome-Based Planning and Evaluation for Public Libraries* (ALA Editions, 2016).
3. See IDEO, *Design Thinking for Libraries: A Toolkit for Patron-Centered Design* (2015), http://designthinkingforlibraries.com; Amy K. Garmer, *Rising to the Challenge: Re-envisioning Public Libraries* (Aspen Institute, 2014); Amy Sonnie, *Advancing Racial Equity in Public Libraries: Case Studies from the Field* (Government Alliance on Race and Equity, 2018), www.racialequityalliance.org/wp-content/uploads/2018/04/GARE_LibrariesReport_v8_DigitalScroll_WithHyperlinks.pdf; and Edmonton Public Library, *EPL Community-Led Toolkit.*

Assessing Your Library's Community-Led Capacity

T
ime to pause for a temperature check. To understand how to increase your library's capacity to engage in community-led work, it is helpful to stop and consider where you are now. In what ways is your organization already strong, and how might you build on or leverage those strengths? Where does your library have the most room for growth, and how can we name and clarify those factors so that change becomes possible?

To analyze these questions effectively, it is important to hold a big-picture understanding of what it means for a library to have high or low organizational capacity for community-led planning. Imagine a librarian (maybe you!) with a passion for community-led work. In some contexts, your efforts might be supported and sustainable; in others, you might invest the same effort and brilliance but feel like you are always pushing a rock uphill. In a high-capacity library, the strengths, skills, and effort of one librarian are amplified throughout the organization, so that the responsibility for community-led perspectives does not depend exclusively on a single person or group. In a low-capacity library, the abilities and work of one person do not spread throughout the organization, isolating them and failing to provide an infusion of organization-wide learning and growth.

Visualizing a high- and a low-capacity model can help further clarify the differences between them. Both have three spheres: the librarian, the library, and the community. The primary differences are in the relationship between the elements.

The low-capacity model looks like a Venn diagram, with overlapping circles for the library and the community. They are literal separate spheres, each with its own goals, cultures, and ways of being. An individual librarian or department with a focus on community-led work stands in their intersection. The more the librarian creates and advocates for community-led practices, the larger the area of overlap becomes. Figure 4.1 depicts this relationship.

FIGURE 4.1

Low-Capacity Model for Community-Led Planning

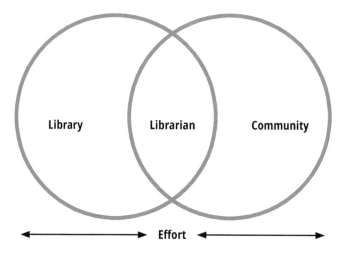

Source: Audrey Barbakoff, "Building Capacity for Equity, Diversity, and Inclusion in Public Library Programs through Community-Led Practices: An Innovation Model" (PhD diss., University of Southern California, 2021), 157.

If you envision a person standing in the center of the diagram, the librarian's core knowledge and motivation are like their muscles. The harder they exercise those muscles, the larger the area of overlap becomes. If the librarian slackens, the overlap decreases, and community and library drift further apart because community-led work is pitted against other library priorities.

This metaphor reveals the core issue with the low-capacity model: it overextends and fatigues the librarian. One person or group must make an ongoing individual effort to overcome the barriers and resistance. They cannot scale programs up beyond their individual capacity for service. Because the librarian's efforts are not amplified or sustained by the organization, when that individual ceases to lead community-led efforts (quite possibly because they have burned out and quit), the organization as a whole loses its capacity for the work.

The high-capacity model, shown in figure 4.2, contains the same elements as the low-capacity model (the librarian, library, and community), but they are arranged differently to reflect the different framing of their relationship. Instead of circles in tension in a Venn diagram, they are nested or concentric circles.

FIGURE 4.2

High-Capacity Model for Community-Led Planning

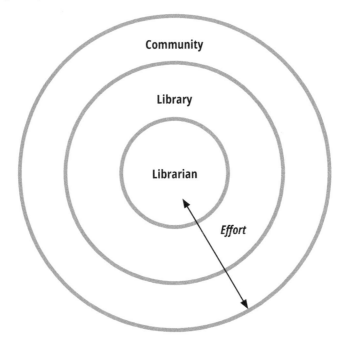

Source: Audrey Barbakoff, "Building Capacity for Equity, Diversity, and Inclusion in Public Library Programs through Community-Led Practices: An Innovation Model" (PhD diss., University of Southern California, 2021), 159.

In this arrangement, the librarian, library, and community are aligned rather than in tension. The high-capacity model sees community goals as the library's priorities, and therefore treats community-led programs and services as efficient and effective ways to accomplish both simultaneously. As a result, in this model, effort is multidirectional and self-amplifying. Now the librarian's efforts increase the overlap between all three circles (envision the "librarian" circle dilating, shrinking the gap between the library and community) by helping the library as a whole grow deeper connections with the community. Additionally, the community can reach back to the library and expand its capacity by inviting librarians to participate in community efforts. Whereas the low-capacity model exhausts the librarian and limits their impact by pulling them in different directions, the high-capacity model allows the librarian's knowledge and motivation competencies to permeate throughout the organization for the benefit of, and in concert with, the community.

What Factors Drive High or Low Capacity?

With this overall understanding of what a high- or low-capacity organization looks like, you may already have begun to think about which model your own library most closely resembles. To turn that into a helpful assessment of your library, it is important to identify the specific factors that lead to its current level of capacity.

Both individual and organizational factors drive overall capacity levels. However, the organization is ultimately responsible for even the individual factors. The organization determines whether or not to allocate the resources and support that librarians need to understand, value, and do this work. If staff throughout the library consistently lack motivation or knowledge, for example, this does not indicate personal failings of individual staff; it reveals that the system is failing to provide some important element.

What are the key factors that determine whether a library is operating on a low- or high-capacity model? In a low-capacity context, staff have low self-efficacy about their ability to engage in community-led work and—more important—they have a fixed mindset about their ability to learn and improve. They work in an organization that limits their autonomy and their time with rigid roles and zero-sum, competing priorities. The organizational culture is rooted more in maintaining hierarchy and "the way we've always done it" than in inclusive learning and growth. Leaders understand success primarily through library-driven outputs like attendance and number of programs, and so undervalue or misunderstand relationship-based outcomes. With community-led services and relationships seen as secondary, this work does not gain widespread organizational traction, and librarians engaged in it become siloed. As a result of the isolation, that librarian's deep understanding of the work and its importance for equity cannot easily spread to others in the organization. Thus, the library's capacity for community-led work lasts only as long as the individual person's motivation to persevere.

When the same librarian enters a high-capacity context, their competencies have a further-reaching impact. Their leaders and colleagues have a deep, shared understanding of community-led work and its role in increasing equity. They all see success as building relationships that help the community accomplish its aspirations. Thus, the library provides staff at all levels with the time, flexibility, and decision-making authority to engage in relationship building. The librarian has a growth mindset, believing in their own capacity to learn and improve, so they are not afraid to enter into unknown situations or deterred when problems arise. This mirrors the culture of the organization, which embraces iteration and human-centered design. The librarian is empowered to collaborate and share learning with colleagues so community engagement becomes infused throughout the organization. The librarian's efforts contribute to increased capacity across the library, both amplifying their impact and making the work sustainable without their constant effort.

Table 4.1 lays out the key factors that differentiate between high and low capacity for community-led planning in an organization.

TABLE 4.1

Differences between Low- and High-Capacity Models

Factor	Low-capacity	High-capacity
Who holds knowledge about community-led work	Individual librarian or department	Shared across organization
Librarian mindset	Fixed	Growth
Definition of success	Outputs defined by library, focused on product	Outcomes defined by community, focused on process
Leadership support	Disinterested	Active, engaged
Culture	Based on tradition, exclusionary	Based on learning, inclusive
Staff time focus	Planning programs	Building relationships
Librarian role	Rigidly defined and siloed	High autonomy and flexibility

Be aware that all forms of organizational capacity, low or high, center on having a person (or people) strongly motivated to do community-led work and skilled in building relationships across differences. Without them, an organization may not have any capacity for community-led work at all. There is no system or structure, however well designed, that can replace the human touch in community-led work. This librarian understands why community-led planning is important and is passionate about how it can lead to greater equity and relevance in the community. They possess the interpersonal and intercultural skills to build authentic, trusting relationships with a wide variety of people and groups, especially from marginalized populations. They engage in self-reflection to understand how their behavior impacts the people they work with and the programs that result. They learn from their experiences to improve their relationships and outcomes.

Do you have someone like this in your organization? (If you picked up this book, that person is probably you!) Community-led work is interpersonal and relational, and so libraries must honor and empower the individual people in their organization as much as they do their external partners. Find these people in your organization—whatever positions they hold—and engage them in your capacity-building efforts from the very beginning.

Community-Led Capacity: Organizational Self-Assessment

The following is a self-assessment you can take to determine where your library stands on the key factors influencing overall capacity. It is fine to go with instinctive responses, as the intention of the tool is to start you thinking about your library's current strengths and growth areas rather than to produce a scientifically valid result. Most libraries will be on a continuum for each answer, so respond with the option that is the best description or most common situation for your library.

1. Who in your organization is actively encouraged and provided with opportunities to learn about concepts like community-led planning, trauma-informed service, and EDISJ?
   a. Most or all people in the organization.
   b. A specified librarian, department, or job class.
   c. Nobody—people who want this have to advocate for it themselves.

2. Many librarians and library workers have not used community-led methods before, and so may not be confident in their current ability to succeed. What mindset do staff have about their ability to learn and improve by trying?
   a. Growth mindset. Staff mostly think that new experiences will be an opportunity to learn and that they will succeed eventually if they put their minds to it.

    b. Fixed mindset. Staff mostly think that learning will be too difficult, and so they do not expect their efforts to result in success.

    c. I don't know.

3. How does your library primarily measure and report on success for programs and services?

    a. We work with community partners to co-create outcomes that demonstrate how much of an impact our services have on participants or communities.

    b. We have some standard outputs we usually report on, like how many programs we offer and how many people attend. We might sometimes try to track outcomes generated by the library.

    c. We don't measure or report on success consistently.

4. What level of support does top library leadership provide for community-led work?

    a. Engaged and supportive. Leadership actively encourages and supports community-led work.

    b. Neutral or disengaged. Leadership does not intentionally put a stop to community-led efforts, but they also do not provide active support.

    c. Opposed. Leaders create almost or completely insurmountable barriers to staff conducting community-led work, or express disapproval.

5. Which best describes your library's culture?

    a. Innovative. My library is open to new ideas, and we see risk and failure as opportunities to learn. We try to create an environment where staff from all positions and backgrounds can contribute and feel safe to speak up.

    b. Conservative. My library is risk averse and strongly bound by "the way we've always done it." Only senior or favored staff have influence over what the library does.

    c. We don't think about our culture.

6. When staff have self-directed time away from a service point, how are they expected to utilize the majority of it? What kind of work is most valued?
   a. Building relationships with community members or partners.
   b. Creating concrete, countable deliverables, like planning individual programs or services.
   c. We don't get time away from service points, or we don't have much direction about how to use our time.

7. How are staff roles defined in the organization?
   a. Autonomous and flexible. People know the purpose of their jobs and have the autonomy to decide how to best accomplish that purpose. We can easily make small adjustments to our schedules or tasks to accommodate community needs, such as attending off-hours meetings. Communication is open between units and individuals, allowing for collaboration.
   b. Rigid and siloed. Each person or job classification has a specific role without much flexibility. Our time is highly structured and tightly managed. There is limited communication between functions or departments.
   c. Expectations around staff roles are unclear.

Results

Mostly *a*: Your library may be operating on a high-capacity model. Congratulations! This likely represents a lot of hard work that has already been done to help meet evolving community needs. Read through the full twelve-step plan, even though you may find that you have already accomplished some of the steps. Identify the areas where you still have more room for growth or where you can build on your existing strengths to take your community-led work to the next level. Focus your energy on those steps first.

Mostly *b*: Your library may be operating in a low-capacity model. Don't worry! Community-led work is still new in many public libraries, and it often represents a significant shift from previous ways of working. It is perfectly reasonable for libraries to begin from a place of low capacity. You have already taken the first steps toward building your capacity by going through this assessment honestly. Now you are more aware of the individual factors where you have the most room to grow and the ones where you may already be doing better than you thought. Plan to follow the entire twelve-step process to develop your capacity.

Any *c*: Any individual question where you selected *c* may indicate an area to prioritize. You may need more information about how your library handles this factor. It could also reveal an area that needs a greater level of change. Read through the entire twelve-step process and identify steps that seem to address this need most directly at your organization. You may wish to begin these steps earlier than the general recommendation.

Most likely, you selected a mix of responses. Go back to the individual questions and reflect on what each one reveals about your library. Where do you currently have the greatest capacity (*a* responses)? Building on your existing strengths can lead to the most rapid and dramatic improvements, creating quick or visible wins that can encourage buy-in across your organization for your change leadership.[1] Where did you select *b*, indicating an area of lower capacity? These may be areas for sustained focus. If you selected any *c*, improvements in these areas may be particularly impactful. How might you get started on them early so that they do not hinder other aspects of your change plan?

Summary

In this chapter, we focused on determining your library's current capacity for community-led work. We presented a high-capacity and a low-capacity model, which are primarily differentiated by the way they construct the relationship between library staff, the library organization, and the community. In a low-capacity model, the library and community priorities are seen as being in tension, requiring the librarian's sustained effort to work in the small area of overlap. In a high-capacity model, the librarian, library, and community are seen as nested and interdependent, working in concert to sustain efforts toward shared goals. Next, we identified specific key factors that contribute to an organization's high or low capacity. Finally, we provided an organizational self-assessment to prompt reflection on how each of these factors currently manifests at your library. The results offer guidance on how you may wish to customize your implementation of the twelve-step plan that will be presented in the following chapters.

NOTE
1. On the benefits of building on strengths rather than fixing weaknesses, see Tom Rath and Barry Conchie, *Strengths Based Leadership: Great Leaders, Teams, and Why People Follow* (Gallup Press, 2008).

The Community-Led Capacity-Building (CoLaB) Model

oLaB is a three-phase, twelve-step model for growing your library's capacity to engage in community-led work. You can think of the phases like the stages of growing a garden. Like a garden, community-led work needs a long season of tending and care before the results are visible. And like community-led work, growing a garden requires a focus on process over product, accepting that you can control what you put in but have only partial power over the ultimately unique results. See "Community Partnerships as a Garden" for more on how Dr. Lenstra developed this metaphor.

A NOTE FROM DR. LENSTRA
Community Partnerships as a Garden

The idea of community partnerships as a garden sprang directly from the research I undertook. In particular, when I talked with Milagros Tanega, branch manager of the Evelyn Meador Branch Library of the Harris County Library in Seabrook, Texas, she shared with me how she cultivated a web of community partnerships to literally start a community garden on the greenspace surrounding her library.

Milagros had been deeply immersed in conversations about sustainable librarianship when she was living in New York, and when she moved to Texas, she brought that ethos to her library leadership. Whenever she would go around the community and talk about the library and its services, she would weave into her elevator pitch the idea that the library would be an excellent host for a community garden, but that they would need help to do it.

Having "planted the seed" of the library as a community-garden facilitator, Milagros then nurtured the seed by building community partnerships around it. Shortly after Milagros shared her vision with the local Rotary Club, one of the attendees—the city manager—was independently approached by a nonprofit seeking to start a community garden in Seabrook. The city manager asked the nonprofit, "Have you talked with the librarian?" To which the nonprofit understandably said no. But having planted the seed in the community, seedlings now started to emerge.

Milagros cultivated those seedings by meeting on a regular basis with this nonprofit. Together they came up with a business plan, figured out the logistical hurdles they'd have to overcome, and successfully got a small grant to get started. They started small with an herb garden (which demonstrated proof of concept), and then expanded outward to encompass a vegetable garden and even a fruit forest. Along the way, more partners got on board, including a nearby middle school that now uses the garden for environmental and culinary education.

Milagros harvests her bounty by celebrating this incredible story of success, which in turn brings more partners to the table, including successful efforts to start a lending library of gardening equipment and a StoryWalk around the garden.

And it all started with planting the seed in the community.

Development of the CoLaB Model

The steps of the CoLaB plan are rooted in the findings of Dr. Barbakoff's study described briefly in the introduction. It identifies twelve factors that significantly influence a library's capacity to engage in community-led work. Once the recommendations were developed, they were arranged into three sequential but overlapping phases adapted from the Burke-Litwin Model of Organizational Performance and Change for a coherent implementation plan.[1] This model describes how transformational and transactional (operational) levers work together to lead to sustainable change, with the main impetus for change coming from the community.

The CoLaB Change Model Overview

CoLaB is made up of twelve steps divided into three phases: inspirational change, transformational change, and operational change. Though the phases are broadly sequential, they should also be seen as overlapping and iterative. The change process will unfold in a unique way for each organization, so it may be necessary to occasionally skip ahead or circle backward to reinforce an earlier change. This is perfectly fine. CoLaB is intended as a guide to be adapted, not a one-size-fits-all plan to be applied strictly.

Figure 5.1 provides a visualization of the CoLaB model. The phases move left to right, but their work overlaps. Arrows indicate that the process is iterative; libraries may need to move freely backward and

FIGURE 5.1
Visualizing the CoLaB Model

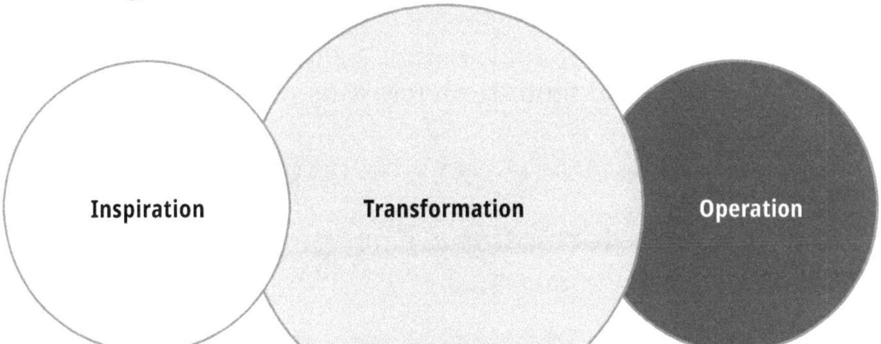

Source: Audrey Barbakoff, "Building Capacity for Equity, Diversity, and Inclusion in Public Library Programs through Community-Led Practices: An Innovation Model" (PhD diss., University of Southern California, 2021).

forward to respond to unique and dynamic situations. The inspirational and operational phases are the same size because they contain an equal number of steps (three). The transformational phase is twice as large, containing six steps and the bulk of the effort. Plan to spend most of your time here.

Phase One: Inspirational Change (Cultivating the Soil)

The three steps in this phase provide the basis for all the others. They are the foundational aspects that should be in place first. You can think of this as cultivating the soil, preparing the ground for healthy growth. The inspirational changes are:

1. Leaders should set clear, measurable expectations for the organization to prioritize and be accountable for EDISJ and community-led work.
2. Provide training on community engagement and EDISJ concepts.
3. Connect community-led programs to broad community goals and EDISJ values.

Combined, these steps provide basic organizational support (by setting an expectation that this work is valued and should happen), foundational knowledge (developing a shared understanding of what the work is), and motivation (creating a clear picture of why the work matters.)

Phase Two: Transformational Change (Planting the Seeds)

These recommendations pertain to changing the landscape—shifts in culture, perceptions, and interactions. Think of this phase as planting the seeds. In this phase, you are sowing seeds and beginning to see where your efforts can grow and be sustained. The payoff may not be immediately visible, but this is where the seeds come to life underground, shifting what you see from soil to plant life. The transformational changes are:

4. Foster a growth mindset about librarians' abilities to learn community-led practices.
5. Develop the psychological safety and open communication needed to support an organizational culture of inclusive innovation.
6. Provide time and space for reflection.
7. Hire and train for interpersonal skills in cross-cultural contexts.
8. Create opportunities for librarians to draw connections between their prior knowledge and experience to community-led work.
9. Learn about the community through relationships as well as data.

Phase Three: Operational Change (Tending the Garden)

These are operational changes to a library's day-to-day activities. The plants have pushed their way to the light, and you continue to water, fertilize, and weed what you've sown. These steps have a clearly visible connection to the desired result. However, they are not very useful without sufficient investment in the earlier phases. You cannot harvest a flower from a seed you never planted or that grew in bad soil. Similarly, do not be tempted to jump straight to the more concrete, operational steps in phase three without first investing in the less tangible underlying work.

Watch Out for the Most Common Pitfall

An oft-cited statistic in organizational development research is that 70% of organizational change efforts fail.[2] Read that again: a full seventy percent. Why? In part, this can happen when the people who are most impacted by the change, and whose cooperation is required to implement it, are not fully invested. You need to create a shared sense of purpose, engage people meaningfully in the process, and support a culture where the kind of work you want to see can actually thrive.

In the CoLaB process, most of the work of creating a shared sense of meaning and buy-in happens during the transformational phase. It is no accident that this is the largest category, containing fully half of the steps (and likely more than half of the time and effort). Yet it is also the work that, in my experience, libraries are most likely to skip. Do not underestimate the importance of this phase. It not only builds buy-in from individuals but also leads to shifts in organizational culture and mental models that make change sustainable.

I understand why focusing on transformational change may not always hold immediate appeal for library leaders. Intentionally shifting culture and surfacing unseen, unspoken patterns can be difficult and slow. This work often does not have a clear finish line or easily measurable result. And the benefits may seem indirect or too far off to be worth the trouble. It is tempting to jump straight to the operational changes in phase three, which are easily observable and directly controlled by management. But it is the messy, intangible work of culture shift that ensures that the operational changes instituted are the right ones, and that they stick.

One way to visualize the importance of semi-intangible or implicit changes is through the Water of Systems Change model.[3] Building on Peter Senge's groundbreaking work in systems thinking, it identifies the six interrelated conditions that need to be in place for meaningful, sustainable change in complex systems (like libraries and their communities). At the structural or explicit level are structural changes like policies, practices, and resource flows such as budget and staff time. Relational changes—think power dynamics, relationships, and connections—are semi-explicit; they are partially visible or often not considered closely. Transformative change is implicit and refers to the mental models people hold. For change to take hold, all three levels must be in alignment. Changing just the policies, for example, without addressing potentially adverse underlying power dynamics or mental models is less likely to have a successful result. Figure 5.2 is a visualization of the inverted triangle of the Water of Systems Change model.

Ignoring or underinvesting in interpersonal and cultural transformational change is the biggest mistake a library is likely to make

FIGURE 5.2
Six Conditions of Systems Change

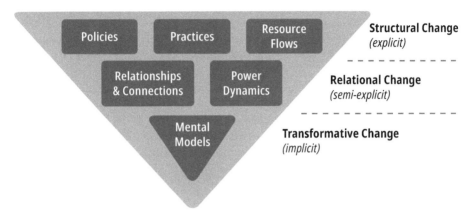

Source: Adapted from John Kania, Mark Kramer, and Peter Senge, *The Water of Systems Change* (FSG, 2018), 4, http://efc.issuelab.org/resources/30855/30855.pdf.

when using the CoLaB plan. The Water of Systems Change model identifies why—because the intangible work of shifting underlying culture and perspective is essential to impactful, sustainable change. Commit to spending sufficient time and energy to accomplish the work in phase two.

Summary

In this chapter, we introduced the Community-Led Capacity Building (CoLaB) model. Libraries of all sizes and locations can use and adapt this implementation plan to grow their own capacity for community-led work. CoLaB has twelve steps distributed across three overlapping, iterative phases: inspirational (cultivating), transformational (planting), and transactional (tending). Libraries should plan to put resources into phase two in particular. Table 5.1 provides an overview of the phases and steps.

TABLE 5.1

CoLaB at a Glance

Phase One: Inspirational Change	
1.	Leaders should set clear, measurable expectations for the organization to prioritize and be accountable for EDISJ and community-led work.
2.	Provide training on community engagement and EDISJ concepts.
3.	Connect community-led programs to broad community goals and EDISJ values.
Phase Two: Transformational Change	
4.	Foster a growth mindset about librarians' abilities to learn community-led practices.
5.	Develop the psychological safety and open communication needed to support an organizational culture of inclusive innovation.
6.	Provide time and space for reflection.
7.	Hire and train for interpersonal skills in cross-cultural contexts.
8.	Create opportunities for librarians to draw connections between their prior knowledge and experience to community-led work.
9.	Learn about the community through relationships as well as data.
Phase Three: Operational Change	
10.	Give staff time, flexibility, and autonomy to build relationships.
11.	Make it everyone's work.
12.	Measure success through relationships.

NOTES

1. See W. Warner Burke and George H. Litwin, "A Causal Model of Organizational Performance and Change," *Journal of Management* 18, no. 3 (1992): 523–45, https://doi.org/10.1177/014920639201800306.
2. Boris Ewenstein, Wesley Smith, and Ashvin Sologar, "Changing Change Management," McKinsey, July 1, 2015, www.mckinsey.com/featured-insights/leadership/changing-change-management.
3. See John Kania, Mark Kramer, and Peter Senge, *The Water of Systems Change* (FSG, 2018), http://efc.issuelab.org/resources/30855/30855.pdf.

Phase One
Inspirational Change

Inspirational change is the first phase of the CoLaB model. The three steps in this phase set the stage for success throughout the process by providing a foundation of organizational support, knowledge, and motivation-enhancing clarity about why community-led work is important. While anyone in the organization can initiate the process, those in formal leadership positions are especially well positioned to support inspirational changes. The steps in this phase are:

1. Set clear, measurable expectations for the organization to prioritize and be accountable for EDISJ and community-led work.
2. Provide training on community engagement and EDISJ concepts.
3. Connect community-led programs to broad community goals and EDISJ values.

Each of these steps is an evidence-based recommendation that responds to one of the findings of the original study. An overview of the findings and recommendations in this phase can be found in table II.1. Read this left to right—for example: Libraries have greater capacity when leaders prioritize EDISJ in community programs. Therefore, library leaders should set clear, measurable expectations for the organization to prioritize and be accountable for EDISJ and community-led work.

TABLE II.1

Relationship between Findings and Recommendations

Finding: Libraries have greater capacity when . . .	Evidence-based recommendation: Therefore, library leaders should . . .
. . . leaders prioritize EDISJ in community programs.	. . . set clear, measurable expectations for the organization to prioritize and be accountable for EDISJ and community-led work.
. . . librarians understand the connection between community-led practices and EDISJ.	. . . provide training on community engagement and EDISJ concepts.
. . . librarians believe that community-led programs are important.	. . . connect community-led programs to broad community goals and EDISJ values.

The CoLaB model is iterative. While starting with the three steps in this phase can lay the groundwork for future steps to succeed, a library may also need to extend or revisit them throughout the process. For example, leadership may need to update or reiterate EDISJ expectations on an ongoing basis. Learning about community-led and EDISJ concepts should be integrated into ongoing training expectations, not offered just a single time. Staff may need additional help with drawing connections to community goals or EDISJ values when a new initiative is launched. Returning to prior steps, or overlapping them with later ones, are not failures of the process. This is a natural part of work that is inherently relationship-based and thus cyclical rather than linear. As you transition into phase two and beyond, continue to reflect on when supports from phase one may need to be refreshed.

Set Clear Expectations and Accountability for EDISJ

What It Means

Libraries build capacity for community-led work when leaders set clear, measurable expectations that the organization will prioritize EDISJ and hold people at all levels accountable. Because community-led planning is a method for putting EDISJ values into action, libraries with a stated EDISJ commitment have strong reasons to use it.

Libraries have the greatest capacity when leaders go beyond supportive language alone—when they moved from lip service to real accountability. While it is important that an organization affirms its belief that EDISJ work is valued, what truly grows organizational capacity is a commitment to consistently providing resources and support, and holding the organization accountable for real results. Leaders should not only voice personal support for EDISJ-enhancing practices; they should also expressly set strategic initiatives, measurable goals, and concrete performance expectations that lead people throughout the organization to actively prioritize this work. Leaders should back these goals up with enough time, support, and budget for staff to succeed in reaching them.

This step comes first because it provides the resources that will be needed for many of the other steps. Leadership is a primary internal driver of change and culture inside an organization.[1] For the subsequent steps to succeed—or even to start—a leader should be willing to invest sufficient organizational time and resources. This happens only if they make EDISJ, and thus community-led work, a priority. If support from those in formal administration roles is not forthcoming, individuals in any role can step up to become the leaders they need within their own span of influence. Returning to the high- and low-capacity models described in chapter 4, supportive leadership is one of the factors that differentiates a high-capacity organization from a low-capacity one.

Exploring the Evidence

This step is rooted in the study finding that libraries have greater capacity for community-led work when their leaders make it a priority for which the entire organization is held accountable. Participants brought up the importance of the role of leadership twenty-eight times across two focus groups. In journals, they wrote that their capacity increased when librarians knew that "their time and efforts are supported by the organization" and that "the variable that seemed to make the most difference was the buy-in of admin." One librarian explained that community-led planning should be part of leadership's broader commitment to the library's EDISJ values, stating that such programming "has the potential to create the environment for more equitable library service and needs organizational support at the Leadership level." However, although study participants agreed almost universally on the importance of leadership, most did not report receiving the level of support they wanted. This leads to an important question: What can you do if your senior leadership is not supportive?

Strategies for Success: Leverage Existing Structures

The specific ways a library expresses leadership support may differ. In the original study, one library found great success in building their capacity by weaving community-led work into their strategic plan. This can be a powerful approach in libraries that actively use a strategic plan and are ready to refresh it. However, in many libraries, this may not be the case. It may be more practical to make stated commitments in shorter-term formats first, like annual goals. Also, while a strategic plan is often guided by senior leaders, many people in the organization may have the power to set goals—they can cover the organization as a whole, a smaller group like a branch or department, or an individual's work. Considering other formal documents, EDISJ can be made an explicit part of job descriptions and performance reviews. Budgets or staffing plans can be designed to provide concrete resources to EDISJ work.

For libraries that do not use any structured plans, or when those leading community-led efforts are not in upper management, writing out clear expectations in a project plan or even an email can be a meaningful action. The important element is that the leader clearly communicates a firm expectation for which staff (including themselves) will be held accountable.

To summarize, a library can use any of a variety of strategies to implement this step, as long as they are clear and actually impact people's work. Some possible strategies include:

- implementing a strategic plan
- setting annual goals (organizational, departmental, individual)
- aligning performance expectations (such as in annual reviews)
- formulating a project plan
- crafting a memo or an email
- allocating a budget line
- developing a staffing plan that specifies time put toward community-led work

In the case study for this chapter, you can see a real-world example of how a library's leadership demonstrated an active commitment to prioritizing community-led work.

Addressing Pitfalls: Unsupportive Leadership

If you are not part of your library's senior leadership, you may be wondering what to do if your director or upper management isn't on board. Does that mean you have to give up before even starting step 1? Absolutely not. Director and senior-level support is certainly helpful, and realistically would make the path forward easier. However, most study participants were able to successfully run community-led programs in their libraries despite reporting only middling levels of support at best, and in a few cases even active opposition. They found—or made—the commitment they needed within smaller parts of the organization, like a department or branch. As their success grew, they could sometimes grow support upward.

Leaders exist at all levels of an organization. In a large system, a department or branch manager can set expectations and allocate some resources for their reports. A group of individual contributors without management positions may be able to band together to advocate for resources and lead this work forward. In a small library, even a single dedicated librarian or two can lead the way. If you are reading this book, the leader your organization needs is probably . . . you! Think about what you can do within your role, and who you might bring along with you as partners in leading the way.

CASE STUDY • Laurel Public Library

Location	Racial demographics	Staff size
Laurel, Delaware (population 15,877—town plus surrounding rural areas)	(for Laurel School District—analogous to Laurel Public Library service area): 69% White, 20% Black, 8% Hispanic, 3% Other	(ca. November 2021): 13 on staff: 5 full-time, 7 part-time, 1 sub.

Located in rural Southwest Delaware, the Laurel Public Library serves "the poorest town in the entire state of Delaware, with a poverty rate of 35.2%, and 42.6% of our kids are on free lunches," according to Wenona Phillips, who has worked at the library since 2006 and who Dr. Lenstra interviewed in 2020.

Former library director at Laurel Public Library Dr. Tameca Jewell Beckett, current library director Gail Bruce, assistant director and head of circulation Wenona Phillips, and Abby Mitchell.

Photo courtesy of Dr. Tameca Jewell Beckett. Date: August 23, 2018.

To transform how the library worked with this high-needs community, Dr. Tameca Jewell Beckett made a firm commitment to equity, diversity, and inclusion. To act on that value, she set the following expectations:

- Library staff strive to meet, or at least connect with, every individual or organization working to make a difference in the community.
- All full-time staff write at least one grant application a year, based on community needs, documented in binders of community information curated by library staff.

Dr. Beckett said these expectations emerged from going to library conferences featuring urban librarians "talking about maker spaces and digital media labs" and then coming back to Laurel and reflecting: "No one can tell me that our community shouldn't be able to have this."

Dr. Beckett says her expectations had become deeply incorporated in the day-to-day practices of library staff when she was out of town on August 21, 2017, the day of a total eclipse. That day, the library "ended up having hundreds if not thousands of people" at an event they sponsored. Dr. Beckett told Dr. Lenstra:

> I did not have a care in the world because I shared how I did everything, because it can't ever be about me. They handled it brilliantly. If you pour into people, and allow them to be their authentic selves, and express themselves, and make them feel cherished and valued, then you don't have to be there.

Here is how Dr. Beckett's expectations were set, and the impacts they had, according to Phillips:

> Prior to 2016, we were that traditional library. Any grants that were done were primarily only by our director, and the rest of the staff didn't have access [to them]. When Tameca Beckett came on as our director in 2016, she had a completely different mindset on what libraries should be doing. One of the first things she did when she started [was have] a retreat. Retreat implies fun, relaxation. It was not that. It was a full weekend of full-time staff getting together and asking, "What is the library? What is our mission?"
>
> She said we should be looking at grants, specifically, because of our unique community needs. She said, "I want each of you to just try to get grants." [In the process of doing so,] we started being fully aware of what our community needs were. She wanted us to engage with our local organizations. We started meeting with different organizations each week.
>
> We would need to write letters [to different organizations and individuals] just to say, "Hey, we appreciate what you're doing in the community." We have a local weekly paper that's called the *Star*, and so one of the things that I would do every week is look through that paper. When I saw different positive things going on in the community—like one of our local teens becoming an Eagle Scout—we'd reach out and write to him with a letter thanking him for what he's doing. It didn't matter who they were, whether they were a politician or just one of our local kids; we were reaching out more, and people's perception of us started changing.
>
> Then, in October 2016, we did the Inspire Community Awards that were a way to get all of the nonprofit/service/resource/faith-based/educator community leaders together [at the library] to say, "Thank you for what you're doing for our town," and we just applauded them. It was truly a red-carpet event. We completely transformed our entire library, and it was just amazing. We did that [event] two years in a row, and when Tameca left, [outside] organizations started looking to us—[when] they had a need, they started reaching out [to us, rather than the library having to be the entity that initiated the relationship].

TAKEAWAYS

1. **There is nothing that a community cannot have due to its size or funding base.** In Laurel, these expectations led to the library being part of everything, from creating a free community fitness trail to ensuring that everyone has access to food daily.
2. **Change takes time and cannot be about any one person.** Dr. Beckett led the way, but ultimately the success of her expectations depended on her ability to step back and let the organization carry the baton forward.
3. **Success breeds success.** As of this writing in summer 2022, the Laurel Public Library secured a Summer Feeding Project grant from Save the Children. That grant was written by Stacy Lane, who joined the library after Dr. Beckett left, illustrating how the culture of shared expectations ripples forward from 2016 to the present.

Summary of Step 1

Leaders in an organization should start by setting concrete expectations for EDISJ in their organizations, with a plan to hold themselves and others accountable. (General statements of EDISJ values or commitments are good, but not sufficient without actionable strategies.) Leaders should be prepared to put organizational resources—such as staff time and budget—behind this commitment. Community-led planning is primarily intended as an EDISJ strategy, and therefore committing to EDISJ lays a foundation of support for this type of work. It is ideal for formal senior leaders to make this commitment because of their influence over organizational culture and resources. However, if this is a barrier, establishing EDISJ expectations at any level of your organization can start to make an impact.

NOTE

1. On change, see W. W. Burke, *Organizational Change: Theory and Practice* (Sage, 2018). On culture, see P. Northouse, *Leadership: Theory and Practice*, 8th ed. (Sage, 2018).

Train for Understanding, Not Procedure

What It Means

Often, one of the first ways libraries try to support community-led planning is through training. Training does have an important role to play—but it may not be the one you think. Libraries often default to procedural or "how-to" training. However, a single training on *how* to conduct community-led planning is unlikely to have widespread impact on its own. Instead, the library should invest in ongoing, conceptual education that emphasizes *why* this kind of work matters.

Procedural training has limited impact because there is no one clear path that all community-led programs follow. Since they respond to the unique needs of their participants at a moment in time, each one evolves in its own way. There are similarities, of course, and underlying models that are broadly applicable, such as the model developed by the Working Together Project.[1] But the specifics of implementation vary significantly. The original ideas come from different sources and address different topics; partnerships can be structured in a variety of ways; the mix of skills, roles, and resources among partners differs; intersectional identities and cultures influence the process. Creating a community-led program requires adapting and responding to these factors, not following a rigid series of steps. An overly concrete step-by-step process is simply not all that applicable in practice.

How do librarians learn the skills to navigate this kind of ambiguity? They need a foundational understanding of the role community-led work can play in achieving equity, diversity, inclusion, and social justice. Understanding the underlying principles of community-led work helps librarians apply them successfully in dynamic and unique situations. To build this mental model, librarians need grounding in ideas like racial and social justice, asset-based community development, trauma-informed service, power and privilege, accessibility, cultural fluency, and human-centered design thinking. These ideas are complex and need to be integrated over time, not in a single training session. Thus, libraries should make a systematic plan for ongoing professional development and education with a focus on community engagement and EDISJ topics. Procedural training on community-led planning techniques is a secondary goal and will likely only be effective if delivered in the context of rich, ongoing conceptual education.

Exploring the Evidence

When I talk to librarians about community-led planning or programs, they often tell me they need training. They will say they do not know how to do this kind of work. Therefore, procedural, or how-to, training seems like the obvious solution.[2] I directly tested this assumption in my study through questions about the types of knowledge and training librarians needed. I was surprised to find that a procedural training approach is, frankly, not very helpful.

How is that possible? I found that if librarians had an understanding of *why* the work was important, and how it was tied to their goals and values, they were willing to learn the *how* along the way. Lack of procedural knowledge simply was not a major barrier. The librarians in the study—all of whom had conducted very successful community-led programs—frequently expressed not knowing exactly how they would proceed at the beginning. They said things like:

"I didn't know how . . . but I did it."
"I'm not trained formally in these techniques."

"I came in not knowing much about community engagement and had to learn a lot."

"How can we do this? Let's just figure it out."

This is not to say that librarians did not need knowledge or training. They just needed a different kind. Instead of procedures, they needed to understand concepts. Conceptual knowledge refers to awareness of the theories, principles, or structures that underpin a practice.[3] The knowledge that led to success was of this kind, especially an understanding of the relationship between community-led practices and EDISJ.

Study participants discussed conceptual knowledge forty-two times across two focus groups. Conceptual knowledge was most frequently raised in the context of emphasizing the importance of the link between community-led planning and serving excluded and marginalized audiences. In their journals, when asked to complete the sentence "For community-led programs to be successful, librarians in our group needed to know or learn . . . ," half of respondents brought up conceptual knowledge of the link between community-led planning and EDISJ.

Librarians want to provide relevant and responsive services to their communities, especially those that have been excluded.[4] When they fully understand why community-led planning is an effective way to accomplish this goal, they are able to find ways forward even in the absence of procedural knowledge. Therefore, libraries should focus on training related to the underlying concepts of community-led planning, such as asset-based community development, human-centered design or design thinking, ACES and trauma-informed service, racial equity, and social justice.

In retrospect, this makes perfect sense. Instruction on the *how* of community-led planning has been easily accessible for many years. One of my favorite guides, the Working Together Project's highly readable and practical *Community-Led Libraries Toolkit*, has been freely available since 2008.[5] If good procedural training were all librarians needed, this approach would already be widespread. Conceptual education, not procedural training, is the key.

Strategies for Success: Consider Context

The primary strategy for success is to take the ideas presented in this chapter and align them with the context of your organization. Libraries can have drastically different levels of resources and types of approach to training. An intensive, custom training plan for all staff might be overwhelming for a small organization, while supporting individuals to attend an existing outside training on occasion as it arises might be too unstructured for a large system.

Consider the resources and norms of your organization in the design of your training request or proposal. How often are staff able to attend trainings? Does your library have a training budget or staff role? Should you look for options that already exist or try building your own in-house? The more closely your plan aligns with the standard practices of your organization, the more likely it is to be adopted.

Be sure to frame your justification in terms of the organization's mission and strategy. If your organization has already made a commitment to EDISJ, you can articulate how the trainings you propose would help the library live up to its promise. If the library has a training plan or budget, find out how resources are allocated and clarify how these trainings can help fulfill the existing plan. In this way, your trainings may be seen as mission-critical, and even potentially as reducing others' workload rather than increasing it.

Addressing Pitfalls: Getting Buy-In

Organizations may hesitate to invest in conceptual education, which carries a higher price tag because it requires an ongoing, systematic commitment rather than a one-time workshop. Additionally, people may at first consider it to be less practical than procedural training. To help win over important stakeholders, emphasize the reasoning for, and benefits of, this type of training.

At first glance, conceptual training may appear to have less direct practical use because the learning is less concrete. However, my research found that nothing could be further from the truth. Providing procedural training without conceptual education is like trying to build a house with no foundation. It is an understanding of foundational concepts that makes practical application possible, especially given the dynamic nature of community-led work.

Organizations tend to over-rely on procedural training, so we may have been conditioned to think of this type of solution first and to return to it even after it has been proven ineffective.[6] Stay the course—focus on conceptual education.

 CASE STUDY · **Anne Arundel County Public Library**

Location	Racial demographics	Staff size
Anne Arundel County, Maryland (population 568,346)	67% White, 18% Black, 8% Hispanic, 4% Asian American, 5% Other	292 on staff: 126 librarians, including 61 ALA MLS librarians

With a county seat in Annapolis, the state capital of Maryland, the Anne Arundel County Public Library (AACPL) serves a mixture of urban, suburban, and rural communities. Throughout these many communities exists endemic "poverty amidst plenty," according to a 2016 report from the Community Foundation of Anne Arundel County.[7]

Given this diversity, the AACPL has sought to create opportunities for library staff to participate in networks and initiatives that focus on transforming how community organizations operate.

These trainings have not been exclusively focused inward—that is, focused on training library staff—but have instead held space open for others to learn alongside the library, and for the library, in turn, to learn along others. These initiatives include:

- the Groundwater Institute, a partnership between the Racial Equity Institute (REI) and Impactive, a coalition of racial equity advocates and organizers
- the Casey Family Programs' Communities of Hope, focused on preventing the need for foster care by supporting families in raising safe, happy, and healthy children

The Groundwater Institute training focuses on the nature and impact of structural racism, and what it looks like across institutions, by examining narratives of racial disproportionality while making use of data to illustrate the systemic nature of racism. When the library brought this training to the county in 2017, not only did they offer it to library staff, but they also opened the training to the wider public. Further, they offered it multiple times and in multiple locations, including online during the COVID-19 pandemic.

This training led to some procedural changes, including the procedure to ask any entity proposing a programming partnership with the library to answer the question "Does this program proposal connect to the Urban Libraries Council's Statement on Race and Social Equity?" Both library staff and community partners reaffirm this statement in their day-to-day practices, communicating both internally and externally the AACPL library's commitments.

This training, and the way it was offered, illustrates the library's general approach to training—which, according to Rebecca Hass, the library's programming and outreach manager, is that

> we all have room to learn and grow. Giving these different opportunities for us as a collective [county] to learn and grow has been instrumental [to us] recognizing the color of poverty.

A second major way the library has trained for understanding rather than procedure is by becoming involved in the Casey Family Programs' Communities of Hope initiative, focused on preventing the need for foster care by supporting families in raising safe, happy, and healthy children. In this program, the Casey Family Programs works with high-needs communities across the country to cultivate and leverage multisectoral approaches to addressing the root causes of childhood inequity by gathering leaders trying to address systemic needs in a particular place.

Since 2015, one of those communities has been Brooklyn Park, located in the north end of Anne Arundel County, and with poverty and racial demographics analogous to Baltimore, which is across the county line. There, with the support of library administration, Brooklyn Park library staff became active, regular participants in the Brooklyn Park Community of Hope process. To learn more about the broader ethos of this process, Rebecca Hass traveled to Gainesville, Florida, to learn about a unique library partnership that emerged because of a Community of Hope process. The library created a new library partnership branch, staffed both by librarians and a family-support facilitator from the local partnership for children.

Although the AACPL did not open a new branch like the one in Florida, the library became a critical part of the Communities of Hope in Anne Arundel County, which after success in Brooklyn Park expanded to other high-needs communities in the county, including Deale, located at the south end of the county, where endemic rural poverty has long affected the life chances of residents.

As a result of participation in these training initiatives, the library staff have transformed how they're seen in the community. According to Janet Raines Taff of the nonprofit South County (SoCo) Connect, even when there is staff turnover at the library, partnerships are sustained due to new library representatives continually coming to Community of Hope meetings. An ancillary impact of supporting library training in this way is that the library is also training the community to see the library in a new way: as an organization vested in and committed to transforming issues related to diversity, equity, and inclusion.

TAKEAWAYS

1. If your library brings in a speaker or training program related to EDISJ, open it up to the wider community. Or, alternatively, offer it twice: once for library staff, and then once again for library staff as well as community members.
2. Be on the lookout for coalitions like those structured by the Casey Family Programs' Communities of Hope framework. Multisector partnerships are becoming more common in the nonprofit and philanthropy sectors, but sometimes you have to seek out a seat at the coalition table.
3. Frame participation in coalitions as a form of training for understanding. You are training those who participate in the coalitions to see the community as a partner in everything the library offers.
4. Don't completely overlook procedure. By doing things like embedding the Urban Libraries Council's Statement on

Race and Social Equity into your program proposal form, you are embedding your library's commitments into your day-to-day practices.

Summary of Step 2

The most effective training to support community-led practices is ongoing conceptual education. Create a regular schedule of learning opportunities related to the underlying principles of EDISJ and community engagement. Examples might include asset-based community development, human-centered design, ACES and trauma-informed service, racial equity, privilege and identity, disability justice, and public participation. How-to trainings on community-led planning techniques may not be effective on their own. If providing procedural training, it should be offered as part of this broader context after a solid foundation of EDISJ concepts has been formed.

NOTES

1. See Working Together Project, *Community-Led Libraries Toolkit* (2008), www.vpl.ca/sites/vpl/public/Community-Led-Libraries-Toolkit.pdf.
2. Susan A. Ambrose et al., *How Learning Works* (Jossey-Bass, 2010); Richard E. Clark and Fred Estes, *Turning Research into Results: A Guide to Selecting the Right Performance Solutions* (Information Age Publishing, 2008).
3. David R. Krathwohl, "A Revision of Bloom's Taxonomy: An Overview," *Theory into Practice* 41, no. 4 (2002): 212–18, https://doi.org/10.1207/s15430421tip4104_2.
4. H. Reid and V. Howard, "Connecting with Community: The Importance of Community Engagement in Rural Public Library Systems," *Public Library Quarterly* 35, no. 3 (2016): 188–202, https://doi.org/10.1080/01616846.2016.1210443.

5. See Working Together Project, *Community-Led Libraries Toolkit.*
6. Clark and Estes, *Turning Research into Results.*
7. Community Foundation of Anne Arundel County, *Poverty amidst Plenty VI: On the Road to Progress for All, 2018* (2019), 6th ed., www.aacounty.org/boards-and-commissions/partnership-for-children -youth-families/forms-and-publications/2018-needs-assessment -poverty.pdf.

Connect to Core Values and Community Goals

What It Means

The first two steps deal with organizational support and knowledge. However, one of the most powerful tools for increasing capacity for community-led work is along a third dimension: motivation. In general, people are motivated to seek out knowledge and make difficult changes when they believe that the subject is important, referred to in the literature as high subjective value.[1] Similarly, Dr. Barbakoff's research found that librarians are motivated to engage in community-led planning when they believe that it is important.

But how can you convince the people around you—or even articulate to yourself—why this work matters? One way is to demonstrate that community-led work helps achieve important community goals and core professional values. Drawing connections between people's values and work goals increases motivation.[2] This step is less about taking a discrete action and more about the language you use throughout all the other steps. Whenever you discuss community-led work, frame it in terms of core values and community goals.

In terms of core values, make a clear connection between the value of EDISJ and community-led work. Equity, diversity, and inclusion is a core value of the library profession.[3] The previous step in this plan already explored the importance of connecting EDISJ to community-led planning in an intellectual or knowledge-based way. This step focuses on clarifying it from a values-based perspective as well. Librarians do not only need to *know* that community-led work and EDISJ are interrelated; they need to *feel* and *believe* that their work makes a difference. Explicitly frame community-led planning as a way of living up to our personal, organizational, and professional EDISJ core values.

Also, draw clear connections between this approach and its impact on community wide goals. Libraries strive to be responsive to their communities.[4] Community-led work is naturally aligned with this aspiration because by definition it involves libraries engaging in partnerships and goals the community believes to be important. When discussing a community-led project, frame it in terms of the importance and impact of the librarian's efforts to the broader community. When librarians can see how their community-led work makes a difference for big issues that matter to those they serve, the importance and value of community-led work becomes clear.

Exploring the Evidence

The importance of subjective value to motivation in the context of community-led capacity was one of the study's strongest findings. In focus groups, every single participant expressed a belief that community-led work is important. In their journals, 78% of participants cited subjective value as their primary motivator. They felt that community-led planning is important because it responds to community, helps the library fulfill its mission, and reinforces EDISJ values.

When librarians described why they were motivated to begin a particular community-led program, they usually saw it as meeting an important community need or aspiration. The specific nature of the aspiration and its programmatic response was different in every case. Some were social justice oriented, while others focused on creating joy, sharing art, or bringing together a divided community through food and conversation. As one of the participants said, "it's not about us. It's about the community." Believing that a program was important to the community motivated librarians to begin, persist, and find creative ways to work around roadblocks.

Participants derived great personal satisfaction from seeing their work have positive impacts on the community. Because the community initiated or collaborated on the program, librarians could feel confident that their work was making a difference, and they found this intrinsically rewarding. They used emotional and figurative language to emphasize this, calling community-led programs "transformative opportunities" and "an amazing experience." They described being "passionate" about or "hungry" for community-led work and said it felt like "magic" or "lightning in a bottle."

Knowing the importance of their work kept librarians motivated even when encountering barriers. As one participant put it, "For those that do community-led work, you do see the benefit. It is hard, yes. And you do see the difference that it makes." The emotional rewards of seeing their work make an important difference led to even greater motivation to continue community-led practices in a self-reinforcing cycle. This cycle likely contributed to making the importance of subjective motivation one of the strongest, clearest findings of this study.

Strategies for Success: Talk, Talk, Talk

In practice, the strong emphasis on subjective value as the main motivator to engage in community-led work is why the CoLaB model places this step in phase one. A highly motivated librarian who believes deeply in the importance of community-led work can lead transformative change in the organization, even in the face of barriers and challenges. Their dedication drives them to lead the learning, growing, and changing described in the next two phases. Their passion helps others around them see the value of this work.

If this sounds like you, then take a moment to appreciate the gift you are bringing. You, yourself, are one of the most important assets your organization has in deepening its connection to community. It may seem obvious to you why this work is important, how it helps the library respond to community goals and uphold core values. Do not assume it is obvious to others. Whenever you talk about community-led work, or about a project or program that is using community-led methods, be sure to draw this connection. Explain how your approach puts EDISJ values into practice. Describe the big-picture community goal or aspiration, and explain how your work (and therefore the library itself) is playing a role. Spread a sense of meaning to everyone you can, as often as you can.

Addressing Pitfalls: Isolation

In the study, all the librarians were highly motivated to engage in community-led planning and believed strongly in its value. But not all of them were in equally supportive environments. When the people around them did not value or understand this approach, librarians reported feeling isolated, disconnected, misunderstood, or even intentionally marginalized. This took a toll, draining their energy and reducing their capacity to do the work they cared so much about.

If you start to feel alone or isolated in this work, refresh yourself by connecting to others who share your passion. While a library operating at its fullest community-led capacity would infuse support and interest through all staff (step 11), you do not need everyone on board at this point. Find a few individuals with a similar perspective and make time to talk with them regularly about your efforts. If you cannot find anyone inside your organization, look outward. There are many librarians doing inspiring community-led work in all sorts of libraries and geographies. We believe in the power of community for our libraries and our patrons—let's not forget how much it matters to our own well-being, too.

CASE STUDY · High Point Public Library

Location	Racial demographics	Staff size
High Point, North Carolina (population 113,019)	45% White, 35% Black, 10% Hispanic or Latine, 7% Asian American, 3% Other	60 on staff: 18 librarians, all with MLIS degrees

On November 19, 2014, the *High Point (NC) Enterprise*, a local newspaper, published on its front page "Hunger in High Point," an article focused on the fact that the city was the second most food-insecure city in America, according to a study by the Food Research & Action Center.

At the same time that local media was shining a spotlight on food insecurity, the staff of the High Point Public Library was trying to reinvigorate its community engagement. The library invited the executive director of the Greater High Point Food Alliance to come in and discuss this issue with library staff, and the library also worked with a local minister to create a weekly community café in the library's foyer—a gathering place for all to come in and have a warm meal. The café grew out of the recognition that individuals experiencing homelessness were already coming to the library as a safe place during the day.

Library director Mary Sizemore said that many of the library staff already knew that food insecurity was an issue because they interact with the public daily. But having the issue publicized and discussed throughout the community created a space for the library to think about engaging in the local food system.

As the library became more involved in the local food system, opportunities emerged to better connect the library's values to the community's core values. Librarian Mark Taylor, who with another librarian started a Teaching Garden at the library in the early 2010s, joined the Greater High Point Food Alliance as an active member. By getting involved with the Food Alliance, Taylor and the library were able to form new partnerships and get even more involved in community conversations.

The library took things even further in 2016, when the city of High Point was looking for a new, permanent location for its farmers' market. It made sense to Sizemore and her staff that the library should be that place. Also that year, Taylor and others active in the Food Alliance started talking about urban farms and community gardens, leading to the establishment of the urban agriculture nonprofit Growing High Point and the Urban Agriculture Committee of the Food Alliance, which Taylor has led.

The library was a key part of strengthening the Local Foods System and Downtown Revitalization: Actions and Strategies for High Point, North Carolina, a technical assistance program funded by the Environmental Protection Agency (EPA). That program focused on renovating the library's parking lot to create a new library plaza. The EPA project was led by the library director, working alongside a local foundation, the Food Alliance, the city of High Point, and the chamber of commerce. These partners, with financial and technical support from the EPA, permanently transformed the library's parking lot into a place beyond cars. The grant proposal stated that "the planned renovation at the High Point Public Library is envisioned as a catalyst for improving health, wellness, and walkability, and building community."

By 2022, the library was central to the community food system in High Point. More recent developments include:

1. The library received a grant from the State Library of North Carolina to join the Charlie Cart Project to better enable local partners from the US Department of Agriculture's SNAP-Ed program to offer pop-up cooking classes at the library's plaza.
2. The library received a $100,000 grant from a local foundation to increase and augment its Teaching Gardens around the library property.
3. The library was a 2022 finalist for the IMLS's National Medal for Museum and Library Service, largely due to its work in community food systems.

The foundation that gave the library $100,000 to increase its Teaching Gardens said in a press release: "This project aligns with our mission of investing in organizations within the greater High Point area that promote improved quality of life by reducing barriers to opportunity. Besides beautifying a highly visible intersection of our community, we are excited that the garden will provide an intentionally designed space for sensory learning, as well as an experiential garden space with therapeutic capabilities for all members of our community."[5]

By aligning community food systems to the library's core values, and doing so in a way that is sustainable over time, the High Point Public Library has cemented its role as a community-led institution.

TAKEAWAYS

1. Stay alert to major community issues and think creatively about how those issues relate to your library's core values.
2. Finding one major issue—like food insecurity—may be more beneficial than trying to work on everything happening in your community.

Summary of Step 3

Librarians are motivated to use community-led planning techniques when they believe this approach is important. You can help people develop a sense of importance by clearly connecting community-led planning to community goals and professional and personal values. You can do this every day by talking about community-led work with a frame of being responsive to community goals or upholding core EDISJ values. When people see how community-led work impacts things they already care about, they will value it more. As a result, they will feel more motivated to engage in it from the beginning, as well as in the next two phases of this capacity-building plan, even if they encounter challenges. If one of the challenges you encounter is isolation, cultivate a community for yourself of people who share your passion and inspiration, wherever they may be.

NOTES

1. See Susan A. Ambrose et al., *How Learning Works* (Jossey-Bass, 2010); Richard E. Clark and Fred Estes, *Turning Research into Results: A Guide to Selecting the Right Performance Solutions* (Information Age Publishing, 2008); and Allan Wigfield, Emily Q. Rosenzweig, and Jacquelynne S. Eccles, "Achievement Values: Interactions, Interventions, and Future Directions," in *Handbook of Competence and Motivation: Theory and Application*, 2nd ed., ed. Andrew Elliot, Carol Dweck, and David S. Yeager (Guilford Press, 2018), 116–34.

2. Clark and Estes, *Turning Research into Results*; J. Eccles and A. Wigfield, "In the Mind of the Actor: The Structure of Adolescents' Achievement Task Values and Expectancy-Related Beliefs," *Personality and Social Psychology Bulletin* 21 (1995): 215–25, https://doi.org/10.1177/0146167295213003.

3. American Library Association, *American Library Association Strategic Directions* (2017), www.ala.org/aboutala/sites/ala.org.aboutala/files/content/governance/StrategicPlan/Strategic%20Directions%202017_Update.pdf; American Library Association, *Equity, Diversity, Inclusion: An Interpretation of the Library Bill of Rights* (2017), www.ala.org/advocacy/intfreedom/librarybill/interpretations/EDI; Christie Koontz and Barbara Gubbin, *IFLA Public Library Service Guidelines* (De Gruyter Saur, 2010), https://doi.org/10.1515/9783110232271; L. L. Thompson and C. Fuller-Gregory, *The Movement toward Equity* (Public Libraries, 2020), http://publiclibrariesonline.org/2020/05/the-movement-toward-equity/.

4. Institute of Museum and Library Services, *Transforming Communities: Institute of Museum and Library Services Strategic Plan, 2018–2022* (2018), www.imls.gov/ sites/default/files//publications/documents/imls-strategic-plan-2018-2022.pdf.

5. High Point Public Library, "Sensory Garden," n.d., www.highpointnc.gov/2563/Sensory-Garden.

Phase Two
Transformational Change

The second phase of the CoLaB model is transformational change. Transformational change refers to shifts in the underlying culture of an organization, including its deeply embedded processes and characteristics.

The steps in this phase are:

4. Foster a growth mindset about librarians' abilities to learn community-led practices.
5. Develop the psychological safety and open communication needed to support an organizational culture of inclusive innovation.
6. Provide time and space for reflection.
7. Hire and train for interpersonal skills in cross-cultural contexts.
8. Create opportunities for librarians to draw connections between their prior knowledge and experience to community-led work.
9. Learn about the community through relationships as well as data.

As in the prior chapter, each step is an evidence-based recommendation that responds to one of the findings of the original study. An overview of the findings and recommendations in this phase can be found in Table III.1. Read this left to right—for example: Libraries have greater capacity when librarians understand and reflect on their skills, abilities, and performance related to community-led practices. Therefore, librarians should have time and space for reflection.

TABLE III.1

Relationship between Findings and Recommendations

Finding: Libraries have greater capacity when . . .	Evidence-based recommendation: Therefore, library leaders should . . .
. . . librarians believe in their ability to learn to conduct community-led planning.	. . . foster a growth mindset about librarians' abilities to learn community-led practices *and* . . . create opportunities for librarians to draw connections between their prior knowledge and experience to community-led work.
. . . leaders foster a culture of inclusive innovation.	. . . develop the psychological safety and open communication needed to support an organizational culture of inclusive innovation.
. . . librarians understand and reflect on their skills, abilities, and performance related to community-led practices.	. . . provide time and space for reflection.
. . . librarians know how to develop and apply interpersonal skills in cross-cultural contexts.	. . . hire and train for interpersonal skills in cross-cultural contexts.
. . . librarians have deep knowledge about their communities.	. . . learn about the community through relationships as well as data.

Transformational change is the largest and arguably most important phase, with the most steps and likely requiring the greatest investment of time. Yet it is also the work libraries tend to de-emphasize or skip entirely. Why? Organizational culture work can seem indirect and amorphous. For example, fostering a growth mindset or psychologically safe work environment does not automatically lead directly to a measurable increase in the number or quality of community-led programs. Changing culture also requires ongoing shifts rather than one-time initiatives. There is no clear, single moment when the work is "done," no box to check off. Maintaining a culture of inclusion, for example, requires ongoing commitment. It may be tempting to try to jump right to the comfortably concrete and direct steps in phase three. Do not do this.

It is essential to commit fully to transformational change for the overall effort to succeed. These seemingly indirect efforts do in fact have a large impact on the outcome. To continue the garden metaphor, think of operational changes like individual plants—when you plant them in a nurturing environment of transformational change, they take root. Trying to make the surface-level changes before addressing the underlying environment is one reason that organizational change efforts fail. You wouldn't plant a garden in poor soil, so don't try to make operational changes without transforming your culture first. To continue the metaphor, you wouldn't plan a palm tree in upstate New York—but perhaps if you built a greenhouse, something as unlikely as a tropical tree would grow even in this unlikely climate.

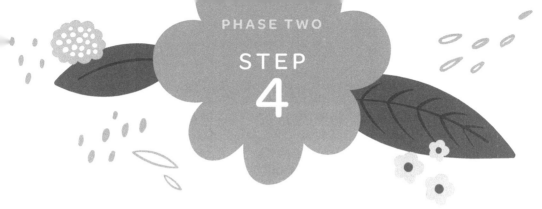

Foster a Growth Mindset

What It Means

Imagine that you have just picked up a guitar for the first time. You put your fingers on the frets, give an exploratory strum, and . . . it sounds terrible. Do you conclude that you're just naturally bad at the guitar? Or do you believe that you'll improve if you practice?

The first reaction—to see your initial failure as a sign of innate and permanent lack of talent—is a fixed mindset. The second scenario, in which you see your ability as something malleable that you can learn to improve, is an example of growth mindset. Growth or fixed mindset is not an all-or-nothing proposition; it depends on context. You can have a growth mindset about your ability to play guitar and a fixed mindset about your ability to do calculus. Carol Dweck's research finds that to a shockingly large extent, perception is reality here: if you believe you can learn and improve, then you can.[1]

A person's mindset impacts how they approach something new or difficult—something like community-led planning. With a fixed mindset, you assume that a mistake reflects your innate intelligence or worth. Therefore, it becomes important to maintain the appearance of success, avoiding tasks where you might fail and refusing constructive feedback.[2] With a growth mindset, because you believe your performance can improve if you work at it, you see mistakes and failures as opportunities to learn. You enjoy taking risks and trying new things, and you can persevere even if they don't initially work out as planned. You aren't ashamed of asking for input to help you do better. As a result, you can focus on learning and improving (mastery orientation), rather than on being perceived as perfect (performance orientation).[3]

In the context of community-led planning, holding a growth mindset and a mastery rather than performance orientation is key to success. Because community-led work is an unfamiliar approach for many libraries and librarians, you may not have strong abilities or much confidence at first. Maybe you're learning a new way of working, at the same time you're meeting new people from a variety of backgrounds and cultures different from your own. All of us will almost certainly make mistakes and encounter failures. To be successful in community-led work, librarians need to have the courage and resilience to keep learning.

How can you foster growth mindset? Dweck suggests several possible methods.

Priming. Prior to any training or new experience related to community-led work, explicitly tell people (including yourself!) that they can learn and improve the skills they are about to use. Let them know that nobody is perfect at the beginning and that we get better with practice and feedback. Really, it is that simple. It is easy for people to start with a fixed mindset without even realizing it, especially at work when we know that our performance is being evaluated. Calling attention to this assumption and countering it from the beginning are powerful.

Normalize learning from failure. Provide regular opportunities to discuss and learn from failures without recrimination. By letting people observe and experience this as a normal part of the organization's way of working, they learn to see mistakes and failure as valuable stepping stones to future successes. This encourages people to focus on what they can learn, rather than on reaching an external performance metric.

Open and inclusive channels of learning and communication. Growth mindset flourishes in organizations where diverse groups of people have opportunities to learn from each other. Staff should be able to share ideas and give feedback regardless of job title. If you are not in a position to influence how the organization communicates overall, don't overlook the value of individual mentoring. Tell a colleague about a time you started out shaky but improved with experience and constructive feedback. Let others see you learn from a problem and try again.

Exploring the Evidence

The finding behind this recommendation was a surprise in Dr. Barbakoff's research. When she designed the study, she posited that low self-efficacy might be a barrier for librarians interested in community-led planning. The participants quickly proved her wrong. It was true that they did not feel confident in their community-led planning skills—for example, one person called their program "a leap of faith," and another described their confidence at the outset as a "2 or 3" out of 10. But that lack of confidence simply did not slow them down.

What was important to them was not a belief that their existing knowledge and skills were perfect, but their confidence that they could learn individually and collectively. They accepted that they might make mistakes and believed they would learn and improve as they went along. They felt it was important to have "confidence that you can learn together, that you will fill in the gaps as they arise" and the "ability to 'put yourself out there' and engage even if not entirely confident or knowledgeable." In short—they had growth mindsets.

Strategies for Success: Look In and Out

It may be easy to slip into a fixed mindset about yourself, or to feel pangs of doubt about your ability to do community-led work well. When you don't trust yourself, trust the people around you. Librarians in the study repeatedly cited their confidence in their partners, or collective efficacy.[4] They believed the final program would turn out well because they could turn to collaborating subject-matter experts and community leaders. They trusted that they would all learn from and teach each other. Just because growth mindset is an internal perspective doesn't mean you have to develop and maintain it alone. When you can't do everything yourself, trust that you all can learn it together.

Addressing Pitfalls: The Fixed Mindset Trap

We live in a culture that often encourages fixed mindsets and performance orientation. From a young age, we may absorb the message that getting good grades, test scores, and accolades matters more than learning. We may also unconsciously come to believe that things like intelligence, talent, and social skills are unchangeable aspects of our identity. Undoing this conditioning is not easy, no matter how much research tells us it is wrong. Keep trying to focus on the joy of shared learning and discovery, instead of on hitting externally imposed metrics of success. For the times when you cannot, seek out partners and colleagues who will remind you how far you've come and how far you can go together.

CASE STUDY · Memphis Public Libraries

Location	Racial demographics	Staff size
Memphis, Tennessee (population 823,667)	45% White, 35% Black, 10% Hispanic or Latine, 7% Asian American, 3% Other	296 on staff, including 80 librarians, 32 with MLIS degrees

Memphis Public Libraries (MPL) strives to empower all members of their community, but to do so they work to build a foundation that supports empowerment and growth among library employees at all levels. MPL has created a number of formal and informal systems and initiatives to create a library system where growth mindsets flourish at all levels, with relationships at the center of personal growth.

Memphis Public Libraries works to lift up those in their sphere of influence, including staff, volunteers, partners, and patrons. But before they can empower all the people connected with the organization, they make a conscious effort to seek out and hire people who will thrive within that environment. Then, using strategically designed professional development, staff are taught to see through the barriers, take risks, and realize their vision for the community. Christine M. Weinreich, executive director of the Memphis Library Foundation, said, "I spend a lot of my time telling library staffers, 'We want you to talk to us about your dreams, for your dreams for your program, your vision, what you believe is the need and in your neighborhood where you work because you know the need.'" She explained that the relationships built in each community led directly to the need to empower the staff in those communities.

Starting internally, the library system has put effort into "getting the right people in place. The right people in the right place has been really, really important. And I think we've done a great job of that," said Lauryce Graves McIver, the library's assistant director of strategic partnerships. The library system has also nurtured relationships with their staff by allowing them to work to their strengths and support additional training in areas of interest.

One example is the manager of the South Branch, Terrice Thomas. "This particular branch manager of our South Branch is so personally involved and engaged in the community as well, and is so energetic about the programming that they offer personal relationships and their promotion of the program through those personal relationships really successfully," said Weinreich. However, Thomas's dynamic nature was fully realized only after the library encouraged her to take part in a leadership program called I-Lead. McIver described the transformation she saw in Thomas after the training: "She's now branch manager and knocking so many balls out of the park. It's unbelievable."

The internal relationships developed confidence in staff members that was translated into building external relationships. South Branch, under the guidance of Thomas, developed online cooking classes with a series of local chefs, which they were able to continue when the library closed due to COVID-19. Weinreich said, "It was so successful. They've done it every other month, all year long. Wow. Yeah. So how they were able to promote

Outdoor Yoga at the South Branch Library of Memphis Public Libraries on Saturday, August 21, 2021. According to the event description, participants could "learn quick techniques you can do to help ease tension with stretching and breathing. Beginners are welcome! Mats are provided to those who need them."

it and get the supplies that were needed to get to go home. And everybody was on Zoom. We've got these great pictures of like, 12- or 13-year-olds."

Another relationship that was built with South Branch was with local yoga teacher June Phillips, who taught their outdoor yoga classes. And that relationship was supported by a relationship with Weinreich at the Memphis Library Foundation, who worked to secure grant funding for fitness programming. "Not everybody can go buy a yoga mat and blocks and strap. . . . We want you [our patrons] to get your hands on it [and] just learn about it . . . [In] our experience . . . if somebody comes to a class at the library to try out yoga, they might go read a book about yoga," Weinreich explained.

"The more we engage with groups who are out in the community, and partner and sit at their table with them, the more we can bring and they can bring to more people and more eyes and introduce people to more of the resource so they can just better the quality of their life, you know, where and meet them where they are with what their interests are?" McIver said.

The growth mindset fostered in Thomas transformed how she works with the community. Other accomplishments include successfully receiving a $10,000 grant from Canadian National Railway to fund supplementary programs at her branch.

Another example of a solid relationship with a community partner enhancing the ability of both parties to empower the community started with a nonprofit called Bridges Youth Action Center, which works to teach leadership skills to youth. "Bridges reached out to me, because, again,

A flyer for the Comeback Stronger Youth Council at the South Branch of Memphis Public Libraries in summer 2021.

it's that personal relationship thing. I know their executive director and the development director quite well," Weinreich said. Several library branches already hosted youth councils, and Bridges saw the opportunity to bring the two programs together to create something even better.

The Comeback Stronger Youth Council empowers youth to engage in conversations with community leaders on issues that impact them directly, such as access to mental health resources. Weinreich explained that the partnership allows library staff "to be trained on truly empowering youth voices, truly having teenagers at the table where decisions are being made." In addition to lifting the voices of the youth, this collaboration contributes to a deeper understanding of community needs among the adult leaders. After piloting the program at five branches, they plan to expand to all branches in the system, empowering youth in all the communities they serve.

TAKEAWAYS

1. Everyone has the potential to grow, and investing in a growth mindset produces dividends both tangible and intangible to the library's bottom line.
2. Try to catalyze on success—when someone or something is successful in one location within your library system, use that success to foster growth elsewhere in your system.

Summary of Step 4

You can start community-led planning from where you are and what you know right now. You do not need to know everything or be good at every aspect before beginning. Instead, cultivate a growth mindset. *Growth mindset* refers to the belief in your own ability to learn and improve with effort. When you make mistakes, consider their lessons, get feedback, and try again in a new way. A simple technique for cultivating a growth mindset is to remind yourself and others that your abilities are not fixed. Other strategies include normalizing learning from failure through open and inclusive communication. Connecting with others can help you trust that you all will learn and succeed together.

NOTES

1. Carol S. Dweck, *Mindset: The New Psychology of Success* (Ballantine Books, 2008); Carol S. Dweck and Daniel C. Molden, "Mindsets: Their Impact on Competence Motivation and Acquisition," in *Handbook of Competence and Motivation: Theory and Application*, 2nd ed., ed. A. Elliot, C. Dweck, and D. S. Yeager (Guilford Press, 2018), 135–54.
2. Dweck and Molden, "Mindsets."
3. A. J. Elliot and C. S. Hulleman, "Achievement Goals," in *Handbook of Competence and Motivation: Theory and Application*, 2nd ed., ed. A. J. Elliot, C. Dweck, and D. S. Yeager (Guilford Press, 2018), 43–60.
4. Albert Bandura, "Exercise of Human Agency through Collective Efficacy," *Current Directions in Psychological Science* 9, no. 3 (2000): 75–78, https://doi.org/10.1111/1467-8721.00064.

STEP

5

Develop Psychological Safety for a Culture of Inclusive Innovation

What It Means

To grow its capacity to center the community, your library needs to foster an organizational culture where staff of all identities, roles, and backgrounds feel safe to share their ideas and perspectives. We refer to this as a culture of inclusive innovation. It means a library where a part-time, frontline assistant will have their ideas listened to and taken as seriously as a senior manager's. Where BIPOC staff and those from excluded groups feel safe to challenge the status quo, try new things, and speak their mind. Where every staff person feels empowered to take risks because they know they are supported and valued, even if they fail.

If you are thinking that your library may have a long way to go here, or at least have some room for improvement, do not be daunted. The foundation of a culture of inclusive innovation is psychological safety—and that is something that can be intentionally built. Coined by Harvard professor and social scientist Amy C. Edmondson in 1999, *psychological safety* refers to "a belief that one will not be punished or humiliated for speaking up with ideas, questions, concerns, or mistakes, and that the team is safe for interpersonal risk-taking."[1]

This foundational sense of safety is essential for all staff—but especially those from excluded backgrounds—to be able to engage fully in community-centered work. Ironically, a lack of psychological safety is most alienating to staff who are part of the communities that libraries most want to reach. Community-centered work is inherently risky. In part, this is because it is impossible for the librarian to know what the outcome of a relationship or partnership will be. On a deeper level, adopting a community-led perspective requires staff across the organization to question internal traditional perceptions of the role of libraries and librarians, and to interrogate deeply ingrained societal patterns of exclusion and systems of power. It also asks practitioners to engage at a deeply personal level, as it requires self-reflection and building real, meaningful relationships. A person who knows that only parts of their identity are welcome at work is not safe enough to do these things sustainably.

Exploring the Evidence: Innovation Requires Inclusion

Dr. Barbakoff, in her research, posited that libraries would have the greatest capacity for community-led work when they had an internal culture of innovation—one where risk-taking and ambiguity were supported, and mistakes or failures were treated as a natural part of the learning process. This proved true: librarians described using innovation techniques like starting with a simple pilot or minimum viable product, learning from the experience in real time, and iterating. They extolled the importance of curiosity, courage, and willingness to break new ground. However, participants also found that simply adopting the methods of innovation was not enough without addressing power structures, bias, and exclusion in the organization. Innovation cannot be separated from inclusion.[2]

Any efforts to develop a culture of innovation must center equity, taking into account hegemonic power structures within LIS and society. Teams are most innovative when staff have complementary skills and diverse viewpoints.[3] BIPOC staff and those from excluded groups have unique lived experiences that can add new ideas, perspectives, and networks. An organization that fails to actively invite the voices of BIPOC, women, gender-diverse people, and other minoritized identities may alienate, demotivate, or exclude their important contributions. Since structural inequity has kept professional positions disproportionately White, inviting BIPOC contributions also means intentionally inviting contributions from frontline and part-time staff. If only White staff and/or degreed librarians have the psychological safety and connections to innovate, then the organization does not truly have a culture of innovation at all. The recommendation to focus on psychological safety emerged because it supports both innovation and inclusion.

Strategies for Success: Make Failure OK

Organizations can take concrete steps to increase psychological safety for staff. Managers can adopt processes and practices that invite ideas from all staff, and then follow them up with prompt, transparent, and appreciative communication, including resources to support implementation. The field of design thinking or human-centered design provides some potential methods for generating, communicating about, and implementing ideas, such as IDEO's *Design Thinking for Libraries* toolkit. Amy Edmondson's book *The Fearless Organization* details many strategies and actions leaders can put into practice.[4]

Less tangibly but of no less importance, leaders can start to destigmatize failure. This might include publicly admitting and learning from their own failures, as well as treating the failures of others as important learning experiences without shame attached. Managers need to demonstrate humility and appreciation. However, this does not mean "anything goes." Managers should immediately address any exclusionary or harmful behavior that impedes the psychological safety of others, including microaggressions.

What if you are not in a position to control the organization's policies and practices? What if you have a manager who punishes failure, or a leader who listens to only a favored few? Try to develop a bubble of psychological safety around you. Organizations do not have just one monolithic culture. Even in fairly small libraries, different groups and teams can have their own microcultures. Start from where you are. If possible, share the importance of psychological safety with your manager or leadership, and advocate for practices that enhance it. If that is not possible, think about who you could trust. Have a discussion about how you can help foster psychological safety with each other. It may help you feel more secure and more creative at work. You may even find that you are modeling the way for others to follow suit.

Addressing Pitfalls: Individual vs. System Focus

This recommendation is about systems. It challenges the *organization* to provide psychological safety as a foundation for building a culture of inclusive innovation. Sustainably increasing organizational capacity cannot be achieved by pressuring individual people to take more risks or open up more. If staff are holding back or resisting, leaders should consider what it is about the culture that's making it unsafe for those staff to fully engage.

Too often, when staff are resistant to changing their way of working, leaders blame the individual without considering systemic causes. It may be easy to say that a person does not want to innovate or change, does not want to be included, or does not want to make the shift to a community-led orientation. Similarly, it may be tempting to chalk up consistent creativity to one person's innovative "spirit"—something that cannot be replicated and does not need external support. In either case, the idea of a culture of inclusive innovation is reduced to policing individual behaviors, which absolves the organization of having to confront systems that may be making some people feel unsafe. Relying on a handful of innovators-in-spirit to carry the whole culture is unsustainable—a recipe for burnout for the innovators and a mess for the organization when they leave. Categorizing individuals as innovators or troublemakers is particularly pernicious because who gets placed in each category may be rooted in bias related to race, gender, age, or other identity. Already-excluded staff can be disproportionately punished and pushed further to the fringes. While individuals can foster more psychological safety and create pockets of inclusive innovation, libraries should look at their systems and structures as a whole rather than putting the onus on individuals.

CASE STUDY · McArthur Public Library

Location	Racial demographics	Staff size
Biddeford, Maine (population 21,504)	89% White, 2.5% Black, 3% Hispanic or Latine, 3% Asian American, 2.5% Other	13.4 on staff: 6 librarians, 5 with MLIS degrees

The staff of the McArthur Public Library strive to work together and to support one another. By creating a culture of collaboration internally, the library develops psychological safety for library workers to experiment with community-led librarianship.

In interviews, library staff told Dr. Lenstra they are not always close personal friends, due to being of different generations and having different personal interests; but they still have a culture of sharing that fosters psychological safety and feeling connected. This culture leads to librarians supporting each other's programs and initiatives.

Danielle Fortin, teen services librarian, said, "I pop into [adult services librarian] Melanie's knitting group, even though I don't knit. I don't have the attention span for knitting—I have tried a lot. But I pop in, and I say hi. And I talk to all her people. And everybody's very excited to see me. And [children's services librarian] Deanna and I would work on paperwork together. I'd sit on the floor by her desk, and she would sit at her desk, and we were just do stuff together."

Fortin shared that she has worked in toxic work environments in the past, and what makes McArthur different is the simple fact that "we all talk to each other, and not just about work stuff, but in a relaxed way," and there are no professional secrets or hidden agendas.

The library director, Jeff Cabral, strives to ensure that library staff are always included in discussions of new initiatives. Of the eighteen communities that participated in this project, the McArthur Public Library was one of the only ones in which all project discussions and deliberations involved library staff from adult, teen, and children's services, as well as library administration.

This culture of inclusion creates psychological safety for library workers to try new things. Even though he didn't completely understand it, Cabral supported Fortin when she wanted to join the advisory board of Let's

Move in Libraries. Fortin is an avid roller derby participant, and she used her connections with this community to bring roller skate maintenance classes to her library.

Similarly, other librarians used connections they had formed with age-friendly Biddeford, community gardening groups, downtown development organizations, and others into library programming.

The ability to experiment with library partnerships and with library partners emanates from a culture in which the psychological safety of library staff is prioritized. If something does not work, it is not seen as a personal failing because there is the recognition that working in a community-led fashion is a library-wide priority.

TAKEAWAYS

1. Fostering psychological safety can start from simple things, like trying to create opportunities for spontaneous conversation and resource sharing among staff.
2. Fostering psychological safety can also come from a culture of transparency, in which staff have opportunities to participate in (and shape) library policies and strategic directions

Summary of Step 5

Psychological safety at work means people feel safe to take interpersonal risks. It is an essential foundation for a culture of inclusive innovation—one where every person on staff, regardless of their identity, lived experience, or position, feels fully empowered to think, voice, and try new ideas. There are a variety of strategies your organization can use to enhance psychological safety, such as destigmatizing failure and implementing inclusive, participatory practices and communications. While there are some things individuals can do to help create psychologically safe spaces for themselves and their colleagues, changing the culture is not the responsibility of individual staff members. When thinking about creating psychological safety for a culture of inclusive innovation, the focus must be on organizational and systems change.

NOTES

1. Amy Edmondson, "Psychological Safety and Learning Behavior in Work Teams," *Administrative Science Quarterly* 44, no. 2 (1999): 350–83, https://doi.org/10.2307/2666999.
2. See Audrey Barbakoff, "Building Capacity for Equity, Diversity, and Inclusion in Public Library Programs through Community-Led Practices: An Innovation Model" (PhD diss., University of Southern California, 2021).
3. Jeff Dyer, Hal Gregersen, and Clayton M. Christensen, *The Innovator's DNA: Mastering the Five Skills of Disruptive Innovators* (Harvard Business Review Press, 2011).
4. See Edmondson, "Psychological Safety and Learning Behavior"; IDEO, *Design Thinking for Libraries: A Toolkit for Patron-Centered Design* (2015), http://designthinkingforlibraries.com; and Amy Edmondson, *The Fearless Organization: Creating Psychological Safety in the Workplace for Learning Innovation and Growth* (John Wiley & Sons, 2019).

Make Time and Space for Reflection

What It Means

Self-reflection is important to community-led work. Understanding your own approach and where your strengths lie (metacognitive knowledge) and thinking critically about how you can continue to improve enhances your learning.[1] And community-led planning is all about learning. With previous steps, you have already begun a learning process to shift how you think about and approach service planning, perhaps radically. Even once you have made that shift, the ongoing process of decentering ourselves and our worldviews, and instead centering communities with a range of lived experiences different from our own, requires constant learning, reflection, and iteration.[2] Where did you do well or make mistakes? How did your actions impact the people around you, regardless of your intentions? If you did harm, what should you do next? What was helpful and effective, and what would you avoid doing in the future? What worked with one partner or community, but was ineffective with another? Asking yourself and reflecting on the answers to these types of questions is central to the self-knowledge and cultural humility you need to develop sustainable relationships with partners.

Exploring the Evidence

In Dr. Barbakoff's research, participants frequently discussed and demonstrated the importance of self-reflection or self-knowledge. This happened no less than thirty-two times in just two focus group conversations. For example, librarians could easily describe their own strengths or gaps in skill and ability. They used that self-knowledge to recruit partners who had expertise that they lacked. Participants talked about how reflection helped them learn from their experiences, thinking honestly about what went well or badly after a program and making changes before the next one.

Participants were also asked to journal about what librarians needed to know or learn in order to successfully engage in community-led work. Sixty-three percent responded with a form of metacognitive knowledge, like knowing their own strengths and weaknesses or being "grounded in self-awareness." They emphasized the importance of being able to hear and learn from honest, unfiltered feedback from impacted communities. They also wrote that self-awareness could enhance staff's ability to cultivate awareness of the community. Every single participant also demonstrated self-reflection—for example, articulating things they would do differently in future programs, or identifying skills they wanted to build.

Because the research took place during the COVID-19 pandemic, many participants had recently experienced library closures. An unintended consequence was that they reported having additional time and space for reflection. This provided an unusual window into the difference that reflection can make. Participants felt that their work had benefited significantly as a result, and they were actively trying to find ways to incorporate more reflection into their work post-pandemic.

Strategies for Success: How to Reflect

By now you may be convinced of the value of reflection, but still wondering how exactly to do it effectively. As metacognition is a frequent subject of study in education research, there are many evidence-backed strategies.[3] Below are a few examples.

Periodic reflection. When people pause throughout a process to consciously understand their performance and articulate their learning, they learn more effectively.[4] Therefore, it is helpful to schedule periods of reflection at multiple points throughout a process, not just at the end. In the context of community-led programming, this could mean scheduling a regular recurring time (such as setting aside some time each week) or building in time based on milestones (such as giving yourself an hour after a partner meeting or a program).

Guided journaling. People's natural inclination to self-monitor differs. Some may find it effective to just sit and think, while others may benefit from a structure that prompts them to reflect, such as filling out a guided self-assessment tool. You may find an existing guided journal product that poses questions you like; you may have a set of questions that are common in your organization; or you may just come up with your own. Managers should be able to help staff formulate good reflective questions as well. If you know that you benefit from some structure, try jotting down three to five questions you can ask yourself regularly. For example:

- What has been most effective in building relationships or making a program successful? Why? What lessons can I take forward with this partner, or in the future for other projects?
- Where am I having trouble? Where could I have acted differently, what do I not understand clearly, or where is something just not working well? What might I do to address these issues?
- What might I/we do next? What opportunities are arising that I didn't see before? What potential issues might arise? Who else can we involve? How do my identity and experience shape my responses here, and what possibilities might I not be seeing clearly as a result?

Dialogue. Reflection does not need to be a solitary activity. It can be effective to engage in dialogue with someone who will ask reflective questions and provide targeted feedback.[5] That can be a manager or a peer; feeling safe to have an open conversation and hear potentially challenging feedback is more important than the other person's formal role. If you prefer to process ideas out loud or find that you are energized by talking with others, consider finding a reflection partner. As with individual reflection, these conversations can be free flowing or structured, depending on what best helps you focus and process.

Restorative space. Our usual spaces for working and living may not always be highly conducive to focused self-reflection. Distractions abound, from a noisy coworker to a messy desk to a looming to-do list, and perhaps most of all from our technology. Finding or creating a space where you can focus can help deepen reflective practices. A recent study on designing restorative spaces unearthed ways that library and museum professionals can reclaim their attention and thus their capacity for focus and self-reflection.[6] It found that attention can be restored not only by being in a restorative space, but also through the process of finding or creating one. One of the results of this study was *The Library Workers' Field Guide to Designing & Discovering Restorative Environments*,[7] which provides tools, techniques, and even a community to help people access such spaces for themselves. Is there a space in your workplace that feels restorative, or that you can adapt to become so? If not, where else might you find or create these spaces?

Addressing Pitfalls: Assuming Reflection "Just Happens"

To do the deep, consistent self-reflection needed for highly successful community-led work, librarians should set aside dedicated time and space. Do not assume that sufficient reflection will happen somewhere, somehow, in a spare moment. In the busy day-to-day with many competing priorities, time to focus and contemplate is likely rare or inconsistent. Though your thought process may be internal and invisible, it still requires scheduled time and space like any other task.

Managers and leaders can play an important role in facilitating access to time and space. Examples include scheduling adequate time off-desk or away from service points, supporting staff in accessing a space conductive to contemplation (which may mean creating appropriate spaces onsite or allowing staff to work offsite), and/ or asking questions or providing tools to prompt reflection. Understand that reflection is essential for your staff to excel at and sustain community-led work and make it a priority.

CASE STUDY · Bigelow Free Public Library

Location	Racial demographics	Staff size
Clinton, Massachusetts (population 15,381)	78% White, 2% Black, 15% Hispanic or Latine, 3% Asian American, 2% Other	5.3 on staff: 2.6 librarians, 1.7 with MLIS degrees

In Clinton, Massachusetts, library director Marie Letarte cultivates space for reflection not only among her staff, but also in her web of community partners.

One of those partners, Chelsey Patriss of the Health Equity Partnership of North Central Massachusetts, described Letarte's approach to library leadership. Describing a successful grant application, she worked with Letarte, Patriss stated that "if [Letarte] had applied for the grant, gotten the grant, done the program, it could have just been a one-off thing. But she was instead willing to follow that grant up by attending meetings, and actually meeting people face to face, and talking about the program, and the impact it had, and throwing ideas around with other people: That was what made it not just a grant program, but a relationship, and a partnership that was sustainable."

This quote from Patriss is notable because it describes the relationships and partnerships libraries cultivate as among the most important outcomes of a program. When librarians work in collaboration with communities, the outcomes are often an extended web of partnerships involving the library.

Letarte excels at "throwing ideas around with other people," as Patriss put it. Creating space for reflecting and imagining how the library got involved in promoting health equity has created space for the library staff she supervises to also reflect and imagine in dialogue with other library staff and in conversation with the community.

Laura Taylor is the community connections coordinator for early literacy as part of the Clinton School District. In our conversation, Taylor discussed the close working relationship she has with Debbie Marini, director of children's services at the library. Taylor and Marini's close collaboration around school readiness builds on the equally close relationship Taylor has with Letarte. In a small-town library, work is often all hands on deck, and Letarte has worked hard to ensure that the culture of reflecting and imagining with community partners also includes her staff.

Taylor said that by "working with the library, it's more of building a community and helping our families realize that there are different places to go to help your child." Taylor discussed that by centering their reflections on their common goals—how to best support young children and their caregivers—she and the library staff have found a great system for imagining what could be done to advance this goal in their community.

TAKEAWAYS

1. In a small library environment, sometimes making space and time for reflection involves extending the space outward to encompass key community partners.
2. Start with the idea that a key outcome of programmatic initiatives is extended relationships and partnerships. This enables you and your library to reflect on to what extent and how the efforts of librarians are working toward the goal of the library becoming more densely woven into the community.

Summary of Step 6

Making intentional time and space for reflection is integral to building capacity for community-led planning and programs. Reflection allows you to build knowledge of your strengths and opportunities for growth, as well as your impact on partners and participants. With this understanding, you can make good decisions about what to sustain and grow, what to stop or change, which relationships to cultivate and how, and what to learn. Schedule regular time for reflection in a restorative space. Reflection may be structured or unstructured, and happen individually or in conversation, based on an individual's preferences. Managers can prioritize reflection by supporting staff with schedules, spaces, and reflective conversations or tools.

NOTES

1. Susan A. Ambrose et al., *How Learning Works* (Jossey-Bass, 2010).
2. M. Caspe and M. Lopez, "Preparing the Next Generation of Librarians for Family and Community Engagement," *Journal of Education for Library and Information Science* 59, no. 4 (2018): 157–78, https://doi.org/10.3138/jelis.59.4.2018-0021; Edmonton Public Library, *EPL Community-Led Toolkit* (2016), https://epl.bibliocms.com/wp-content/uploads/sites/18/2015/08/EPL-Community-Led-Toolkit-Final-EXTERNAL-Web.pdf; John Pateman and Ken Williment, *Developing Community-Led Public Libraries: Evidence from the UK and Canada* (Ashgate Publishing, 2013); Working Together Project, *Community-Led Libraries Toolkit* (2008), www.vpl.ca/sites/vpl/public/Community-Led-Libraries-Toolkit.pdf.
3. Ambrose et al., *How Learning Works*.
4. Ambrose et al.; M. T. H. Chi et al., "Self-Explanations: How Students Study and Use Examples in Learning to Solve Problems," *Cognitive Science* 13 (1989): 145–82, https://doi.org/10.1207/s15516709cog1302_1.
5. Ambrose et al., *How Learning Works*.
6. Beck Tench, "Designing Restoration: Protecting and Restoring Our Attention through Participatory Design" (PhD diss., University of Washington, 2022).
7. See Beck Tench, *The Library Workers' Field Guide to Designing & Discovering Restorative Environments* (2022), restorativelibrary.org.

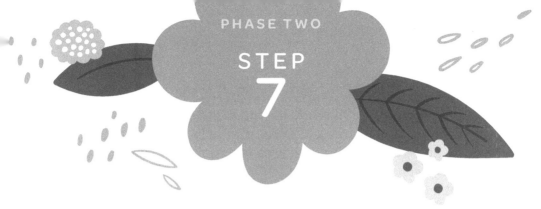

Prioritize Interpersonal Skills and Cultural Humility

What It Means

To be successful in community-led programs, librarians need to know how to develop and apply interpersonal skills in cross-cultural contexts. As we explored in step 2, community-led work requires skillful navigation of complex interpersonal dynamics in diverse groups and ambiguous situations. All community-led programs require building and maintaining relationships. "Hard" skills like subject-matter expertise are less important than "soft" skills like listening, collaborating, and communicating.[1] This is especially true when partners hold marginalized or excluded identities, particularly if they are different from the librarian's own. Librarians need the cultural humility and fluency to decenter themselves, understand unspoken systems of power and privilege, be aware of impact over intention, and recognize and repair bias or harm.

Knowing that interpersonal skills and cultural humility are essential, how can libraries and librarians build them? There are two primary possibilities: training existing staff to grow their skills, and hiring new staff who already have them. Many librarians do not receive sufficient training in cultural and interpersonal skills, so an employer-sponsored program may help fill this gap.[2] However, a one-time training is unlikely to be effective in building librarians' ability to understand and apply a set of interpersonal and intercultural skills in a variety of dynamic contexts. A better approach might be an ongoing program of regular training, including both training on specific skills and education on broad concepts like cultural competence and relationship building.

Another method—one that can be implemented in tandem with staff training—is to make cultural and interpersonal skills a major factor in hiring decisions. A competency-based hiring approach that values candidates' interpersonal and intercultural skills, from both their formal education and lived experiences, may result in a workforce that is both more diverse and more culturally competent. Their skills may then translate into more inclusive programs and services for the public.[3] Of course, relational skills are not stagnant. Even staff who enter the organization with high skill levels should be supported with the ongoing training described above.

Exploring the Evidence

Librarians participating in Dr. Barbakoff's research saw cultural and interpersonal skills as paramount. Especially when sharing power with partners holding marginalized or excluded identities, they emphasized the need to "decenter themselves" even when they were the ones initiating a connection or facilitating a convening. They also cited a lack of interpersonal skills and discomfort in cross-cultural contexts as a barrier. For example, they or their colleagues sometimes held back from engaging deeply out of "fear of doing or saying the wrong thing or contributing to more collective harm." Some noticed that colleagues were intimidated by the idea of cold-calling, or initiating a conversation with a new person or organization. The librarians who were engaged in successful community-led work focused on building and maintaining relationships in a variety of cultural contexts, with people holding a wide range of identities. They recognized the importance of prioritizing and continually developing their ability to do so.

Strategies for Success: Competency-Based Hiring

One part of this recommendation is to make cultural and inter-personal skills part of the hiring process. In practice, how might a library do this? One possible avenue is competency-based hiring. Competency-based hiring entails developing a job description that aligns with the skills needed to excel in a role, and then evaluating candidates (and later, employees) against a rubric of these skills.[4] For example, University of Arizona Libraries developed a competency-based weighted matrix for hiring and evaluating librarians. It included specific, observable interpersonal skills such as managing relation-ships and intercultural skills such as valuing diversity. By naming the specific cultural skills needed to serve your community effectively, and making those a formal piece of the criteria for hiring and evalua-tion, libraries may be better able to recognize the value of applicants' lived experiences and the skills they have built as a result. While not a panacea, this may result in a more equitable and inclusive hiring process, and thus staff that more closely represent the community they serve.

Addressing Pitfalls: Implicit Bias

If strong interpersonal skills and the ability to apply them in cross-cultural contexts become key criteria for hiring and evaluation in an organization, there is a danger of bias. BIPOC staff, women, and others holding marginalized identities may be judged less favorably or more harshly than their performance warrants.[5] Awareness of these biases is a first step in combatting them. When possible, involve diverse teams in decisions around hiring and promotion so that one perspective does not dominate. For accountability, audit your hiring, promotion, and evaluation decisions on a regular basis. Is alignment increasing between the demographics of your staff and the communities they serve, at all levels? Is there evidence that BIPOC staff, women, or others of any marginalized identity are consistently receiving more critical feedback, lower reviews, less appreciation, or fewer resources and opportunities? Establishing an audit cycle allows libraries to understand the impact, not only the intent, of their policies and practices. If there is little or no measurable improvement in this alignment, then bias may be impairing your library's ability to serve its community well.

CASE STUDY · Harris County Public Library

Location	Racial demographics	Staff size
Harris County, Texas (population 2,127,996)	28% White, 19% Black, 43% Hispanic or Latine, 8% Asian American	362 on staff: 125 librarians, all with MLIS degrees

Even though he supervises a staff of hundreds that serves one of the largest communities in Texas, if not the nation, Edward Melton, who directs the Harris County Public Library, based in Houston, makes a point of practicing cultural humility every day.

Celeste Bleu has seen this humility in action. She now works as assistant manager responsible for adult programs at the system level, but when she first started working at the library, she did not have a college degree. Nonetheless, according to Bleu, "every time [Melton] saw me, he said, 'You can do it, you're going to library school, you're a librarian, you don't have the title yet, but you are already a librarian.'" Melton helped Bleu finish her undergraduate degree, becoming the first in her family to do so, and continued to inspire her to get her library degree and to become active in the Texas Library Association.

This ethos permeates the Harris County Public Library. "That model of leadership at the top, it's the model of the leadership within each branch," said Melinda Brinkley, assistant branch manager at the Fairbanks Branch.

During COVID-19, with many staff working from home, many staff felt isolated. Bryan Kratish, the library's manager of outreach services, said that when the pandemic hit, he made it a priority to jump on Zoom at least once a day with all his staff to flatten the hierarchy and to give everyone a space to talk as peers. Kratish also helped develop a mentorship program, allowing staff to build skills and grow as individuals.

This same structure shapes how the library works with the community. One of the library's strongest partners is the Harris County Public Health Department. Linda Stevens, head of the library's Programs, Partnerships, and Outreach (PPO) division, said joining community coalitions has been one of the most effective ways to get to know local community actors and figure out how to most effectively work with them as equals and co-creators. She said, "What has really helped me is that there is in our area a coalition called Healthy Living Matters. And the goal of that coalition is to reduce childhood obesity. From that, not only can I connect with all of these great resources in the health department, but I'm connecting with the food bank, and I'm connecting with the schools and all of these people in the room that are really supporting a lot of the same goals. So that has been a big for us. That's where we started the Summer Meals [program], from working on that coalition."

By seeing everyone within the organization as having expertise and things to contribute, the library also sees everyone in the community as having expertise and things to contribute. That ethos enables library staff to go to community coalition meetings not only to do library outreach, but also to learn, listen, and contribute to community conversations in ways that bring about community solutions.

TAKEAWAYS

1. Prioritizing interpersonal skills and cultural humility can be done both internally to a library organization and externally with community members and partners. Doing the former can lead to the latter.
2. Coalitions can be a great way to build relationships and to put interpersonal skills into practice. Creating mechanisms to get library staff to these coalitions can be a catalyst to community-led librarianship.

Summary of Step 7

Libraries should prioritize interpersonal skills and cultural humility for their staff so that librarians engaged in community-led programming will be able to build and sustain essential relationships and collaborations in a variety of cultural contexts. Your library can do this through training, hiring, and performance evaluation. Training should be ongoing rather than one time, and it should support both concrete skill-building and foundational concepts. Hiring and evaluation should be competency based and should value lived experience. To avoid implicit bias or paying lip service to these concepts without real change, your library can hold itself accountable by auditing their hiring and promotion decisions and performance reviews.

NOTES

1. Fiona Blackburn, "Community Engagement, Cultural Competence and Two Australian Public Libraries and Indigenous Communities," *IFLA Journal* 43, no. 3 (2017): 288–301, https://doi.org/10.1177/0340035217696320; J. Bryson, and B. Usherwood, *Social Impact Audit* (South West Museums Libraries and Archives Council, 2002).
2. On lack of sufficient training, see M. Caspe and M. Lopez, "Preparing the Next Generation of Librarians for Family and Community Engagement," *Journal of Education for Library and Information Science* 59, no. 4 (2018): 157–78, https://doi.org/10.3138/jelis.59.4.2018-0021; Eric P. Lashley, "The Level of Community Engagement in Texas Libraries," *Texas Library Journal* 93, no. 3 (2017): 78–79; and L. Mestre, "Librarians Working with Diverse Populations: What Impact Does Cultural Competency Training Have on Their Efforts?," *Journal of Academic Librarianship* 36, no. 6, (2010): 479–88, https://doi.org/10.1016/j.acalib.2010.08.003.
3. Paul Jaeger and Renee Franklin, "The Virtuous Circle: Increasing Diversity in LIS Faculties to Create More Inclusive Library Services and Outreach," *Education Libraries* 30, no. 1 (2007): 20–26, https://doi.org/10.26443/el.v30i1.233.

4. R. Huff-Eibl, J. F. Voyles, and M. M. Brewer, "Competency-Based Hiring, Job Description, and Performance Goals: The Value of an Integrated System," *Journal of Library Administration* 51, nos. 7–8 (2011): 673–91, https://doi.org/10.1080/01930826.2011.601270.
5. Marianne Bertrand and Sendhil Mullainathan, "Are Emily and Greg More Employable than Lakisha and Jamal? A Field Experiment on Labor Market Discrimination," *American Economic Review* 94, no. 4 (September 2004): 991–1013; Paula Cecchi-Dimeglio, "How Gender Bias Corrupts Performance Reviews, and What to Do About It," *Harvard Business Review*, April 2017, https://hbr.org/2017/04/how-gender-bias-corrupts-performance-reviews-and-what-to-do-about-it.

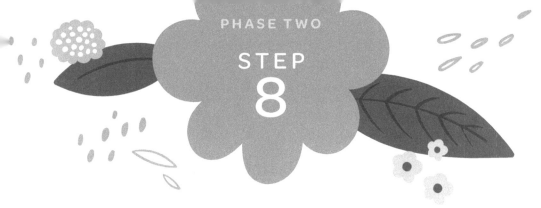

Apply Prior Knowledge

What It Means

Diving into something new when you do not feel confident in your ability can be challenging. Low self-efficacy reduces people's motivation to learn and experiment because we are, understandably, worried about failing.[1] Since many librarians have little or no experience with community-led processes in libraries, it is perfectly normal to feel unsure when starting out. This step is about how to cope with an early lack of confidence so that it does not get in your way.

Connecting prior experience to this novel situation helps you see that you are not really starting from scratch. You almost certainly already have some skills, knowledge, and experiences that have prepared you to do community-led work. You simply may not have applied them at libraries.

Think about times you have worked on a team to accomplish something you cared about. These could be at a prior job or in a different industry, or from your personal experiences. Have you played on a sports team? Then perhaps you have learned how to identify different roles that align with each person's strengths so the whole team can function at its best. Volunteered for a committee in a faith community, or helped plan a family reunion? You may have learned to balance leading and following, deciding when to listen and when to speak. You may have forged consensus across differences to reach a common goal. Do you love to cook? You might have knowledge that can help you build relationships with others in your community with the same passion.

Connecting prior knowledge not only makes people feel more confident, but it also may improve their skills. Prior knowledge is important to developing mastery because we assimilate new learning and novel experiences in the context of what we already know.[2] Having an experience to refer to or rely on may make it easier to understand and apply the elements that really are new. Consciously connecting your prior experiences to the work you want to do now can build your confidence and help you apply the skills you already have. It shows you that you know more than you think you do.

Exploring the Evidence

In Dr. Barbakoff's research, librarians tended to have limited experience with and low self-efficacy for community-led planning, which was in alignment with the literature.[3] Librarians in the study overcame their initial low self-efficacy by effectively connecting their prior knowledge to the novel experience. They were able to articulate how the skills and knowledge they gained in other domains prepared them to do community-led work. These connections increased their confidence in their own abilities.

What participants did feel confident about was their ability to learn, improve, and eventually succeed. (This relates to the earlier recommendation on growth mindset.) The primary reason they gave for this confidence was their prior knowledge and experience. Several people shared work or personal experiences from outside of libraries that they felt had prepared them. For example, one person said, "I approach a lot of my job at the public library just like I'm working in the student health center at a university. . . . It's just a different way of looking at it." People described drawing confidence from their prior learning in areas as distinct as business and art. Despite the fact that some of these experiences might appear to be very different from library work, participants were able to reflect on the lessons learned from those situations and apply them in libraries. This is a metacognitive skill, which relates back to the finding that self-reflection is very important to building capacity for community-led programming.

Strategies for Success: Cross Contexts

Once you have grown your confidence by thinking through how your prior experience relates to community-led work, you can help your colleagues do the same. In general, people tend to find it difficult to apply knowledge from one domain to a very different context.[4] As one librarian in the study wondered aloud, "How do we get others to look at their personal experiences and start with what they know?"

Helping others consider their prior knowledge in a new context is a powerfully simple act. It is difficult to do alone, but fairly easy to do together. And it can make a significant difference in people's confidence and motivation. Simple prompts can be very effective in helping people activate prior knowledge. For example, in a training, an instructor can assign people to write or discuss how their prior work or personal experiences might relate to community-led programming. The trainer may also engage in elaborative interrogation, asking "why" questions to prompt librarians to draw on their own prior knowledge for context. A peer or manager can ask similar questions informally. Perhaps even just reading the examples at the beginning of this chapter got you thinking about your own prior experiences in a new way.

Addressing Pitfalls: This One Is Pretty Safe

Every chapter has a section on addressing pitfalls, so it seemed confusing to omit it here without explanation. But I have yet to encounter any serious downsides or dangers in this step. I would simply advise you not to be overly pushy in your questions. If someone says they really do not have any applicable experience, let it go. They may be resisting for other reasons that are best addressed in a different step. Or they may privately reflect on what you asked at a later time.

Harkening back to the recommendation about psychological safety, people may be unable to talk about their experiences openly if they or their cultures are not fully accepted, and if they are not safe to express their authentic selves at work. The point is not to get an answer, but to encourage people to think about the question.

CASE STUDY · Rutherford County Library

Location	Racial demographics	Staff size
Rutherford County, North Carolina (population 68,772)	82.5% White, 10% Black, 5% Hispanic or Latine, 1% Asian American, 1.5% Other	10 on staff: 3 librarians, 1 with an MLIS degree

Engle Troxler works for the Rutherford County Library, located in the foothills of the Appalachian Mountains. The county has a poverty rate around 20% and is classified as among the most economically distressed in the state of North Carolina. Troxler stated, "We all just have to work as a team. There are too few of us at the library for us to be able to have separate responsibilities."

Library director April Young illustrated how the practice of pooling resources works when she told us that "our IT librarian was doing some research on the internet and saw hydroponic gardening at a library in Georgia. He brought that to me, and he said, 'I think that we can do some hydroponic gardening.'"

Young then reflected on how something like hydroponic gardening could fit into both what the library was already doing and what the community was doing. The idea of growing food at the Rutherford County Library emerged from the confluence of the interests and backgrounds of a number of different library staff members:

- A bilingual (English/Spanish) librarian collaborated with a Spanish-speaking colleague to do a Latin cooking series to introduce cooking from another culture with healthy, fresh ingredients.
- The IT librarian had been working on starting a library makerspace and thinking about creative ways that the library could support making things.

- The marketing and programming coordinator had used her deep knowledge of the community to connect with the head of a local health foundation, who had started providing the library with funding and other resources to support health.
- The library director had been thinking about the walking path behind the library as a space for a garden.

The different staff of the library pooled their resources, ideas, and contacts to come up with the idea, and the library director then went to physically adjacent offices of the NC State Extension offices to see if they had interest in working with the library around hydroponic gardening. As Young put it, "It snowballed from there."

With funding from the health foundation, and with expert insights provided by the office extension, the library secured three hydroponic towers that were then used at multiple library branches, as well as by community partners, to grow food.

According to Hannah Bundy, the horticulture agent for the Rutherford County Center of the extension, the partnership with the library works well because the library is willing to take risks and think unconventionally about things like getting the library dirty during gardening programs.

> Doing gardening classes in that type of environment [the library], we've definitely had to brainstorm to make sure we're not making a mess, but also making it where people aren't restricted with what we're trying to do. And we know that kids like to play with dirt. [The library's IT specialist and makerspace coordinator] Kenneth [Odom] has been really great about not making it so stringent. He is creative about it, and he has fun, which has made it an enjoyable thing on my end as well. Whereas other partners that I've worked with, I feel like I've come into their space, and they're like, "Oh, wait, you have dirt!!" I've never really felt that from the library.

The relationship with the extension office has become so central that library director Young has been invited to join the advisory board of the local extension office. Young said that is huge because she felt that, during her first few years working on health promotion at the library, she and other staff spent a lot of time reaching out and suggesting things to partners.

Now, she said, that has started to shift: the extension comes to the library with ideas, the hospital reaches out with virtual program ideas, and other libraries in the area reach out to suggest partnerships.

You may be able to walk a similar path in your library, starting by talking with your colleagues about their interests. Try to find both common interests and intersections of diverse interests, and then use those commonalities to build momentum. Pool your connections to draw on existing community resources, including both expertise and financial support. As you build momentum, eventually a turning point will come, and others will begin to initiate partnerships with you.

TAKEAWAYS

1. Everyone has skills they can contribute. Becoming community-led includes harnessing the fact that all library staff are also part of different communities that can be woven into the library.
2. Finding ways to support library workers applying prior knowledge can be as simple as creating opportunities for conversation and resource sharing.

Summary of Step 8

Drawing on your prior knowledge from experiences outside the library can help raise your confidence in your ability to do community-led work. You can ask yourself to think or write about the skills you've gained in other situations, and how they prepare you do to community-led work now. You can also do the same for the people around you, just by asking some simple questions. You know more than you realize!

NOTES

1. Albert Bandura, "On the Functional Properties of Perceived Self-Efficacy Revisited," *Journal of Management* 38, no. 1 (2012): 9–44, https://doi.org/10.1177/0149206311410606.
2. See Susan A. Ambrose et al., *How Learning Works* (Jossey-Bass, 2010).
3. See John Pateman and Ken Williment, *Developing Community-Led Public Libraries: Evidence from the UK and Canada* (Ashgate Publishing, 2013); and Working Together Project, *Community-Led Libraries Toolkit* (2008), www.vpl.ca/sites/vpl/public/Community-Led -Libraries-Toolkit.pdf.
4. Ambrose et al., *How Learning Works*.

STEP

9

Build Community Knowledge through Relationships

What It Means

In order to conduct community-led programming effectively, librarians need to know about their communities. Some community information is factual and can be looked up—for example, data that can be found in existing sources, like census data about community demographics. Other information can be gathered, such as what organizations exist in the community and what type of work they do. But some knowledge—from the perspective of community-led work, the most important knowledge—can be learned only through relationships. What aspirations, needs, and values do people share? How do various organizations feel and think about each other, and what are the connections between them? How do people's lived experiences and the community's history shape the perceptions and actions of a diverse range of residents?

Building a robust understanding of community through relationships means treating interpersonal and intrapersonal knowledge as valid. This may feel uncomfortable at first, as it challenges Western colonial and Enlightenment assumptions that the only meaningful knowledge is observable, factual, objective, and measurable. Figure S9.1 visualizes the difference in epistemology between commonly used and community-led frameworks.

FIGURE S9.1
Epistemological Framework Contrast

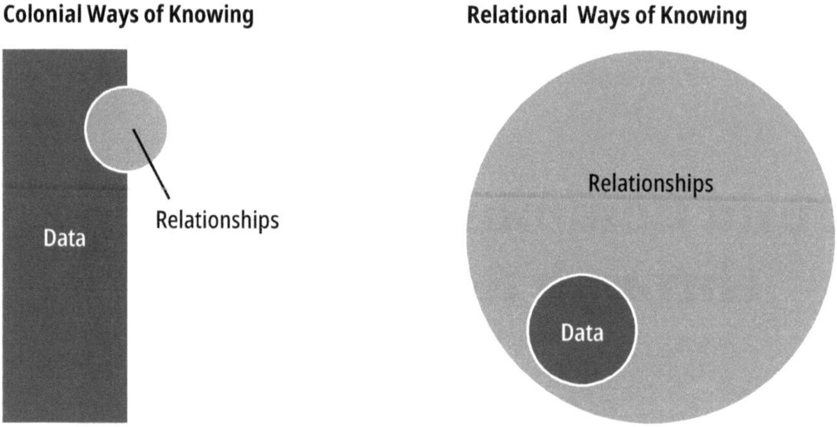

Colonial Ways of Knowing   **Relational Ways of Knowing**

In the way we have often been conditioned to understand what counts as knowledge, we primarily value a narrow, linear slice of the world that can be considered objective data. Relationships are treated as sources of knowledge only when they provide data that cannot be located elsewhere. By contrast, in a community-led framework, we see relationships as the primary source of knowledge because we value people's experiences, subjective perceptions, cultures, and interconnections. Measurable data still plays a role in understanding our communities, but which data matters and what it means is understood within the context of relational knowledge.

Taking time to connect with the people and organizations in your community, particularly those led by and representing BIPOC and other systematically excluded groups, is not separate from or less important than gathering data from the census or the school district. Joining coalitions, attending community meetings, contributing to planning community events, and sitting down one-on-one with community leaders are all ways of learning important things about the community that cannot be ascertained in any other way. Unlike statistics, which can be looked up as needed, meaningful relationships cannot be initiated and discarded on demand. Therefore, library staff need to invest consistently in building and sustaining community relationships to hold deep community knowledge.

Exploring the Evidence

Librarians in the study believed strongly in the benefit of community knowledge for a variety of reasons. When asked to journal about what librarians need to know in order to conduct community-led programs, more than half of participants identified knowledge about their community. This finding aligns research showing that library school professors believe that community knowledge is one of the most important influences on library students' capacity for family engagement.[1] One participant summed up their vision of community knowledge up by saying that librarians who want to conduct community-led planning need to

> know your community. Know its history and demographics. Learn about the needs of the community. Learn what other groups/orgs are working in the community. Learn who the leaders of the orgs and community are so you can collaborate in program planning. Learn what meeting spaces are available to use that are convenient for the community to attend. Ask questions and really listen to what community members express and what they need help with.

Why was this knowledge so important to participants? First, they wanted to make their programs and services relevant to their patrons. They wanted to know more about what people in the community were thinking and feeling so they could support services that were interesting and meaningful. For example, one participant described seeing a map of local artist studios. They said, "This light bulb went off when I looked at that map and I said, 'Wow, we have a lot of artists in our little neighborhood.'" That realization sparked a collaboration with local artists from underrepresented backgrounds that was deeply relevant to that library's diverse user population. Librarians thought that learning about their community helped them avoid making assumptions, and instead respond to who was actually in their service area and what they really wanted.

Librarians in the study also said they needed to know about the organizations that could be potential partners in developing programs, services, and spaces. One participant said that identifying the right partner allows for better connections to the audience of focus because that organization "is on the front line, has an understanding, . . . has the connections, is the trusted messenger." Participants said they used community mapping to help them avoid duplicating the work of other organizations. They also saw this understanding as important to equity, as they could honor and uplift the work that marginalized groups were already doing.

Strategies for Success: Community Assessment and Asset Mapping

Community assessments and asset mapping (sometimes also called community network mapping) are experiential methods that build systematic knowledge about community, including its demographics, social and organizational networks, and people's strengths and aspirations.[2] These are appropriate learning strategies for community-led work because not only do they lead to useful knowledge about community, but they also establish that knowledge within an asset-based frame or mindset.[3]

Community assessment in this context refers to efforts to understand and describe the community.[4] This can include paper research (such as looking up demographics and reading community-created documents) as well as asking people about their aspirations, needs, or opinions through conversations or surveys. The Libraries Transforming Communities method developed for the ALA by the Harwood Institute for Public Innovation in 2015 is an example of a community-assessment tool developed specifically for library use.[5]

Asset mapping is a type of community assessment. It refers to a process of systematically identifying positive elements and resources within a community.[6] There are six primary types of assets that can be mapped: individual people, grassroots associations, local institutions, physical space and infrastructure, local economy, and local culture.[7] These are often represented visually, either on a literal geographic map or in a concept map. (A supplemental spreadsheet or database may be helpful for organizing detailed information, such as contact information or brief descriptions of organizations' services.)

FIGURE S9.2
Sample Asset Map Template

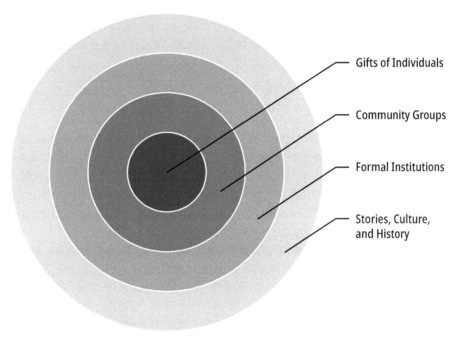

Gifts of Individuals

Community Groups

Formal Institutions

Stories, Culture, and History

Figure S9.2 shows a simple version of one possible way to organize a conceptual asset map.

Asset mapping is generally not effective when done in isolation.[8] To lead to effective change, libraries must take the next step of engaging with the people and organizations they identify, working to build relationships that collectively mobilize those assets and reveal others. Thus, the recommendation to engage in community assessment and asset mapping does not imply a paper exercise. The full realization of this recommendation includes doing research to identify individuals and organizations doing work in their own communities and then reaching out to those organizations to engage in deeper learning and relationship building. Without this relationship element, an asset map or community assessment would provide incomplete and less meaningful knowledge of the community because it would not reveal implicit knowledge such as people's hopes and emotions.

Addressing Pitfalls: One-Time, Unsustainable Efforts

While a periodic in-depth community assessment project is a good thing, the core of building knowledge through relationships is small, frequent connections. Libraries should prioritize and make time for community conversations on a regular basis, not only when they are part of a large, unwieldy process that cannot be sustained as part of everyday operations.

To be effective, relationship-based learning efforts need to be repeated and sustained. For people to share honest, authentic insight with you, they need to trust you; that trust is built by showing up for the relationship in an ongoing way. Additionally, community learning itself is ongoing work because communities continually change and evolve. Libraries should therefore make a regular practice of community learning through relationships. The benefit of this work even goes beyond what you learn in the moment. Done right, it builds the very relationships that will become the foundations of your community-led planning efforts.

 ### CASE STUDY · Gail Borden Public Library District

Location	Racial demographics	Staff size
Elgin, Illinois (population 144,597)	40% White, 5.5% Black, 47% Hispanic or Latine, 5% Asian American, 2.5% Other	144 on staff: 30.7 librarians, all with MLIS degrees

If you walk into the office of Miriam Lytle, director of community services and program development, you'll see on her wall a detailed map of the communities served by the library. That is intentional. Around 2010, the library dramatically changed its service model, moving from a library-based model to a community-based one, organized around the idea of staff members whose primary responsibilities would be to work with different sectors of the community outside any of the library's three service locations. Those staff members are supervised by Lytle, who uses maps and data extensively to identify needs and to tailor library services to them.

Mapping at the library is more than knowing who lives where. Lytle said so much of her work is driven by a combination of tacit and implicit/intangible knowledge. The library does keep a database of contact information for different partners, but so much of their knowledge of those partners and the subsequent assets are in the heads of library staff. Lytle said one of the library's ongoing challenges is balancing the desire to codify that knowledge into maps and databases without losing the implicit and intangible, creating space for staff out in the community to work responsively with community partners without the idea that "this has to fit into the database," constraining that work.

As Lytle said, "If you really have the right intention, of reaching deep [into the community], and you have an open hand, and partnerships, [the results of your work] will be exponentially explosive, and powerful to a point that you can't even imagine." In other words, the library's data-driven approach is also people driven, with the recognition that people can't be reduced to data points. To be sure, data is critical to the library's approach. However, they make the data work for the people, rather than make the people work for the data.

Building up the people to do this work requires ongoing maintenance. Lytle said that an annual staff retreat for the employees in her division always includes speakers with exercises, and that they always try something new to create space for staff to think differently about their work with communities. She also tries to bring in different sectors—most recently, individuals from the hospice sector—to build relationships with library staff.

Lytle said, "What I expect from the staff is not to give us the 'same old, same old.' We want them to be creative, supercharged, enthusiastic, connected people. And my goal is to empower them to be their best selves, bring their best game, and really fly."

This work is driven by asset mapping, and the premise that everyone has assets that can be combined to improve communities. As Tish Calhamer, the library's community engagement manager, said, "Going back to asset-based community development, I tell my team that everybody can lead from where they are and you bring to your job certain gifts. Don't worry about the gifts you don't have—someone else might have it, and if we don't have that gift at all, then that's just something that maybe we look towards hiring in the future." Similarly, Lytle said, "I think from an administrative point of view, the key is to find people who can really plug in to that niche you're trying to reach. Whether that is a staff member that you're hiring, or a partnership that you're working with, that affinity group concept carries over to your staffing." In other words, asset mapping applies both to library staffing decisions as well as partnership decisions—in both cases, the goal is to build from strengths and to identify areas for strategic growth.

Striving to make these assets visible helps the library reframe things from "library services" to "community services." As Tina Viglucci, the library's manager of Hispanic services, said, "I think it's really nice for people to see organizations working together. Sometimes they don't know who's who and, that's fine. It's fine. We're all just doing something for them to be able to participate in the program and I think it becomes transparent to them if it's [one library partner] doing the workshop or if it's [another library partner] doing the workshop, or if it's the library, because we're all there. At the end of the day, we just want people to see that there are people in the community that can support them."

Nonetheless, from an operational perspective, knowing what the library is contributing can be critical to the bottom line. Lytle talks about how they started using all these logic models and ROI (return on investment) models to make the invisible visible. The end result has been that the library is seen as central to nearly anything going on in the community it serves. For instance, Calhamer said, "Last year, just my division alone had a return on investment of almost $5 million of value that we returned to the community in terms of volunteer hours." To illustrate this further: during the COVID-19 pandemic, the library was unable to have its huge number of more than seven hundred volunteers come into the library to do onsite work. So the library encouraged those volunteers to instead work for local food banks, which were in dire need of more hands on deck. This redeployment of library volunteers came about from years of work to map assets internally and externally, and then to put those assets together to positively impact communities, on an ongoing basis.

TAKEAWAYS

1. Think creatively about how you can map or assess the heterogeneous assets that exist in your library and in your community, including volunteers, partners, and library staff themselves.
2. Don't let asset mapping become a straightjacket—use it as a catalyst to propel library staff to work nimbly and creatively with communities to develop new community services.

Summary of Step 9

Community-led planning requires librarians to have deep knowledge about their communities. Reading documented information and data like community demographics is only the surface layer. Much of the most essential information—such as what people think, feel, and experience, and how they relate to each other—is built through community relationships. Community assessment and asset or network mapping are some of the relational tools that can help you learn about your community. However, it is important not to see the tools as large, one-off investments of time. Instead, use them flexibly to empower regular, ongoing relationship building and conversation with systematically excluded communities.

NOTES

1. M. Caspe and M. Lopez, "Preparing the Next Generation of Librarians for Family and Community Engagement," *Journal of Education for Library and Information Science* 59, no. 4 (2018): 157–78, https://doi.org/10.3138/jelis.59.4.2018-0021.
2. John Kretzmann and John McKnight, *Building Communities from the Inside Out: A Path toward Finding and Mobilizing a Community's Assets* (Center for Urban Affairs and Policy Research, Northwestern University, 1993); David Coghlan and Mary Brydon-Miller, eds., *SAGE Encyclopedia of Action Research*, s.v. "Asset Mapping," by Deborah Puntenney (SAGE, 2014).

3. Fiona Blackburn, "Community Engagement, Cultural Competence and Two Australian Public Libraries and Indigenous Communities," *IFLA Journal* 43, no. 3 (2017): 288–301, https://doi.org/10.1177/0340035217696320; Coghlan and Brydon-Miller, *SAGE Encyclopedia of Action Research*, s.v. "Asset Mapping"; David Coghlan and Mary Brydon-Miller, eds., *SAGE Encyclopedia of Action Research*, s.v. "Asset-Based Community Development," by Kenneth Reardon (SAGE, 2014).

4. University of Kansas Center for Community Health and Development, *Community Tool Box* (2020), https://ctb.ku.edu/en.

5. See Harwood Institute for Public Innovation, *A Step-by-Step Guide to "Turning Outward" to Your Community* (2015), www.ala.org/tools/librariestransform/libraries-transforming-communities/resources-for-library-professionals.

6. Coghlan and Brydon-Miller, *SAGE Encyclopedia of Action Research*, s.v. "Asset Mapping."

7. Kretzmann and McKnight, *Building Communities*; Coghlan and Brydon-Miller, *SAGE Encyclopedia of Action Research*, s.v. "Asset Mapping."

8. Coghlan and Brydon-Miller, *SAGE Encyclopedia of Action Research*, s.v. "Asset Mapping."

PART
IV

Phase Three
Operational Change

The third phase of the CoLaB model is operational change. Operational change refers to the tangible practices of an organization, or how it accomplishes its work.

The steps in this phase are:

10. Give staff time, flexibility, and autonomy to build relationships.
11. Make it everyone's work.
12. Measure success through relationships.

As in the prior two sections, each step is an evidence-based recommendation that responds to one of the findings of the original study. An overview of the findings and recommendations in this phase can be found in table IV.1. Read this left to right—for example: Libraries have greater capacity when librarians believe that community-led projects will succeed in building relationships. Therefore, libraries should develop tools and practices to measure success through relationships. Two of the three steps in this phase respond to aspects of one finding.

TABLE IV.1

Relationship between Findings and Recommendations

Finding: Libraries have greater capacity when . . .	Evidence-based recommendation: Therefore, library leaders should . . .
. . . the organizational structure empowers all staff to engage in community-led processes.	. . . give staff time, flexibility, and autonomy to build relationships . . . *and* . . . make it everyone's work.
Librarians believe that community-led projects will succeed in building relationships.	. . . measure success through relationships.

It's finally the section you (or maybe your manager) have been waiting for since page 1. Operational changes are the obvious shifts we make in things like schedules, job duties, budgets, written policies, and formal evaluations. These come last not because they are unimportant; they are essential to providing staff with the resources they need to do the work. They come last because, in order for these changes to be sustainable, they need to be aligned with the culture of the organization. Operational changes that are not connected to culture can feel arbitrary and forced, causing them to be ineffective.

If you have followed along with this book, you have already spent considerable effort on building an organizational culture where these concrete changes can take root. You have built up rich soil where the seeds of transformation can grow. Because of that, some of these operational changes may seem obvious, and you may have already naturally begun to shift your work in this direction. This is a good sign that the operational changes will be sustainable—they clearly align with the culture you have been intentionally building. If you encounter strong resistance to any of these changes, it may be a sign that you need to go back to a previous phase to strengthen culture shifts.

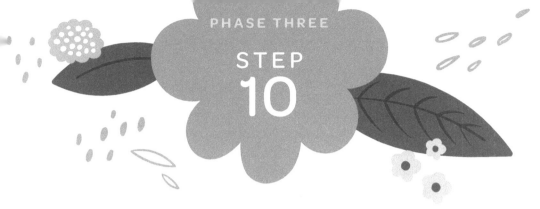

STEP

10

Give Staff Time, Flexibility, and Autonomy to Build Relationships

What It Means

What resources are most important to librarians trying to conduct community-led work? While budget and physical space are helpful, the most needed resource, by far, is time. Because community-led work is inherently relational and building relationships is an ongoing process, it makes sense that it requires a significant, sustained investment of time.[1] Additionally, community-led work leads to new approaches and results, so it requires consistent learning and adaptation, which also take time. However, time is often in short supply in library work. Staff generally need to cover service points at set times and support a variety of programmatic priorities.

Not only do staff need time; they need time paired with flexibility and autonomy. For example, giving staff additional off-desk time in a strictly scheduled way (say, they are scheduled for community-building activities every Thursday morning) is not highly effective. In order for staff to use the time to build relationships, it needs to be spent in ways that are convenient for the community or partner they are trying to reach. Grassroots coalitions may meet on evenings or weekends; reaching informal gathering spaces may require travel time; a key community leader may not know their availability far in advance. All this requires staff to be able to be flexible about when and where their work takes place. Staff also need the autonomy to make decisions in the moment about how to structure at least some of their time, so they can commit to meeting people where they are without unnecessarily lengthy approvals.

The need for staff autonomy also extends beyond managing their own schedules. Once librarians are in the field with their communities—for example, at a community meeting or gathering—they need the autonomy to engage in partnerships on behalf of the library. When an inspiring idea bubbles up and the librarian can see how it aligns with the library's goals and resources, they should be able to express interest and enthusiasm in the moment. An opportunity to say yes (or at least "probably") spontaneously can help build goodwill and rapport. As the circumstances and relationships evolve, the library staff involved should still be empowered to make changes. Needing to check back with a manager before every small decision or even before suggesting a possibility stifles the conversation, bogs down the timeline, and impedes or even halts relationship building.

Giving staff sufficient autonomy does not mean that managers can have no say. It's reasonable that final approval of a large endeavor would need management permission before proceeding to avoid conflicts of time or resources. It's also reasonable to expect staff to keep their managers updated on what is going on and what resources are needed, and to alert them to any potential issues. However, the manager should serve in the role of coach, helping to identify and remove barriers, not in a role of command-and-control. The person who has built a relationship with the partner community or organization is the one best positioned to make decisions about if and how the library should be involved in a particular initiative. If a staff person is given the responsibility of representing the library in the community, then they should also be entrusted with the authority and autonomy to build and act on community relationships.

Exploring the Evidence

Librarians in the study saw time as extremely important and one of the largest barriers they faced to engaging in community-led work.

The topic of having enough time was mentioned thirty-nine times across two focus groups and listed as a key need in more than half the journal entries. While other resources were mentioned, participants gave multiple examples of being able to work around limitations in budget, materials, space, or supplies. They found partners with the needed resources, applied for grants, and scaled programs down, among other strategies. "There are just these little ways that you can start to expand your capacity by not what I can do, but what my partner and I can accomplish if we're working together," said one. Essentially, librarians could find a way to get anything except more time.

Why is time so essential? Study participants gave two main reasons. Most obviously, they needed the time to conduct a collaborative, community-led planning process, which is complex and often has a long timeline. More important, though, they needed time to develop relationships without an expectation of an immediate concrete output. Librarians said they needed time to build relationships for their own sake, without an expectation that the relationship would always lead to a program or initiative. As one person said, "It's worth the investment of time, even though you can't guarantee a deliverable." They said it was essential to spend time "just being an observer participant, and then seeing what comes out of spending time with the [community] group." Investing in relationships for their own sake was even more important with excluded and marginalized populations because of the need to build trust. Librarians needed the time to build authentic, trusting relationships—not only transactional ones meant to lead to a predetermined output within a set period.

Strategies for Success: Start Where You Are

It is no secret that time is a scarce resource in many libraries. Simply keeping the doors open and the service points staffed can be a struggle. For libraries to sustain community-led work, it is important that they treat community-led planning as a shift in the way they do their existing work, not as a separate new activity layered on top of a full schedule of library-centered programs, services, and initiatives. The idea is to transform our current work to be more community-led, not to add more work. Try identifying something you are already doing or planning to do—something like planning next season's programs, creating a strategic plan, or designing a space—and consider how to do it in a more community-led way. Give yourself permission to do fewer things, and invest more time in them.

Becoming more community-led is a process, not a binary. If time is a limitation, start small. Use the time you do have to focus on building authentic and trusting relationships with excluded communities. Relationships are the foundation for all community-led planning, and they are the source of its transformative power, so this is not the place to skimp. Reduce your time commitment by engaging in fewer, smaller initiatives at first. Many people are able to grow from small successes. Once you can demonstrate that your methods have connected new groups with the library in meaningful and innovative ways, even on a small scale, you can use this success to advocate for more staff time. As your capacity grows, you can iterate to create larger and more visible successes. You may be able to use those bigger successes to advocate for yet more staff time and resources, creating an increasing cycle of success and investment.

Addressing Pitfalls: Trust Your Team

Sometimes, library staff time and autonomy are limited not because of unavoidable operational conflicts, but because of overly strict policies and procedures. Managers need to trust people to make good use of their time. In order to build the relationships that underpin community-led work, librarians not only need enough time, but they also need the commensurate authority and autonomy to make decisions about where and when to be present.[2]

Outside of scheduled desk shifts or operational needs, managers should avoid restricting librarians' ability to flex their schedules or work location, or requiring onerous layers of approval to do so. Such limitations can hamper librarians' ability to engage with the communities the library most wants to reach. Similarly, managers should trust their staff with the authority to make at least some decisions on behalf of the library once they are in community spaces. If librarians are given the responsibility of developing community partnerships, then to be successful, they also require the authority to make decisions and commit resources to make those partnerships successful. Strict policies that do not account for the unique needs of the community are no substitute for trusting your team.

CASE STUDY · Bethlehem Area Public Library

Location	Racial demographics	Staff size
Bethlehem, Pennsylvania (population 114,175)	56% White, 9% Black, 30% Hispanic or Latine, 3% Asian American, 2% Other	34 on staff: 8 librarians, all with MLIS degrees

Josh Berk, the library director of the Bethlehem Area Public Library in the Lehigh Valley of eastern Pennsylvania, is most known at the national level for his work on mental health training in libraries.[3]

Berk said he wishes he and his library also got recognition for many of the other amazing initiatives that his library has helped bring about, nearly all of which emerged from him giving his staff the time and authority they need to build relationships.

Across the Lehigh River is the library's South Side Branch, led by Janine Santoro. Berk created a structure that enabled Santoro and other South Side Branch staff to meet once a month with a group of community activists to discuss how they could work together to increase access to gardening and other equipment. Those series of conversations led to the launch, first, of the Southside seed library, and second, of the tool library, which includes shovels, cultivators, socket wrenches, and more available for checkout.

A similar culture of collaboration flourishes at the library's main branch. M. Rayah Levy shared the innovative structure she and her partners have developed to enable the library to offer yoga and qi gong classes on a regular basis for years, with yoga classes offered starting in 2008 and qi gong starting in 2018.

The library does not have the budget to pay these presenters, so instead, Levy worked with the Friends of the Library and with Berk to create a structure wherein people who come to classes are invited but not required to make a suggested donation to the Friends of the Library, which in turn pays the yoga and qi gong presenters, both of whom see their library classes as vital forms of outreach that enable them to reach a more diverse array of individuals than they do in any other settings where they offer their classes.

A final manifestation of Bethlehem's approach to giving staff time and authority to develop relationships centers around the library's bike-share initiative. One of the library's longstanding partners is the local health bureau, or local health department. The library started working with the health department around an effort to increase access to services to individuals experiencing homelessness. A public health nurse offered basic services to these individuals at the library.

Based on that success, Berk empowered a former library staff member who was passionate about agriculture and food to start working with the health department around a project to make the library a pickup point for a local community-supported agriculture initiative subsidized by the health department such that low-income residents could get food for free—with the added bonus of the health department offering free popup cooking classes on how to prepare the food in the boxes.

This initiative in turn led to the library being part of a community conversation on how to increase access to bicycles, particularly for those who are without other means of transportation. With funding from the local hospital, Berk empowered his circulation manager to go to meetings led by the health department in which the library and health department worked on the nitty-gritty details of how to start checking out bikes from the library.

The initiative was a success, and circulation manager Dawn Fritz attributed success in large part to Berk's hands-off approach. Berk enabled Fritz the time and authority to build this relationship so that the partnership came together successfully.

TAKEAWAYS

1. A library that supports mental health is also a library that supports staff autonomy, and trusts library workers to use their expertise to develop community partnerships successfully.
2. Delegation is part of success. Enabling library staff to play to their strengths and think creatively about how to solve problems can lead to unexpected solutions to tricky issues.

Summary of Step 10

To be successful in community-led planning, staff need time to build authentic, trusting relationships with excluded communities. Some of that time can be spent on co-creating specific initiatives, but most of it should be dedicated to simply building and sustaining relationships without pressure for a deliverable. In addition to having enough time overall, librarians need the autonomy to make decisions about where and when to spend that time in order to meet communities where they are. Managers should trust their employees to make decisions about how to allocate their off-desk time and avoid imposing excessive red tape. When time is limited, you can avoid making more work by reimagining existing processes or programs to be community led, rather than adding new ones. It is okay to start small. Demonstrating small successes may make it easier to obtain resources to scale up, creating a cycle of capacity growth. Doing fewer things but investing enough time in them can be more impactful than trying to do small pieces of everything at once. Give yourself permission to slow down.

NOTES

1. Jeff Dyer, Hal Gregersen, and Clayton M. Christensen, *The Innovator's DNA: Mastering the Five Skills of Disruptive Innovators* (Harvard Business Review Press, 2011); Edmonton Public Library, *EPL Community-Led Toolkit* (2016), https://epl.bibliocms.com/wp-content/uploads/

sites/18/2015/08/EPL-Community-Led-Toolkit-Final-EXTERNAL-Web .pdf; Dave Muddiman et al., "Open to All? The Public Library and Social Exclusion: Executive Summary," *New Library World* 102, no. 4/5 (2001): 154–58, https://doi.org/10.1108/03074800110390626; John Pateman and Ken Williment, *Developing Community-Led Public Libraries: Evidence from the UK and Canada* (Ashgate Publishing, 2013); S. Surette, "The Challenge of Evaluating Community-Led Work." *Feliciter* 59, no. 5 (2013): 13–15; Working Together Project, *Community-Led Libraries Toolkit* (2008), www.vpl.ca/sites/default/files/Community-Led -Libraries-Toolkit.pdf.
2. G. C. Hentschke and P. Wohlstetter, "Cracking the Code of Accountability," *Urban Education*, Spring/Summer 2004, 17–19.
3. Josh Berk, "Mental Health Training in Public Libraries," *Public Libraries*, January 5, 2015, http://publiclibrariesonline.org/2015/01/ mental-health-training-in-public-libraries/.

STEP

11

Make It Everyone's Work

What It Means

Community-led planning is a team sport. This is true internally as well as externally. Staff throughout the organization need to understand and be able to engage meaningfully with community-led work, regardless of job title, duties, or positional power. In general, transformation in organizations is most successful when everyone shares responsibility and opportunity for innovation.[1] When community-led work happens in a silo—when only a few people in the organization are formally assigned to do community-led work, and only they are supported in accessing education around community-led topics and ideas—the capacity of the organization as a whole is severely limited.

In fact, frontline employees with no regular planning responsibilities may be among the most important staff to engage. Given that such staff are more likely than librarians or managers to be BIPOC or belong to other marginalized communities, these workers may be most likely to have lived experiences and relationships that form the foundations of community-led work. It is extremely important, however, that these staff members are engaged in a way that is not exploitative. They must not be required to provide additional, uncompensated invisible labor due to identity or role. This is true for all BIPOC workers and others holding marginalized identities, but it is especially important since frontline employees are likely to be among the lowest paid in an organization. Make it safe for staff to share and engage if they choose to do so, and compensate them fairly for their valuable contributions.

Exploring the Evidence

Library directors often ask Dr. Barbakoff what the ideal organizational structure is for a library to engage in community-led work. Is it better to have a dedicated position or team assigned to community engagement and partnerships because this ensures time and resources are available? Or is it better to embed community-led work into many existing jobs to avoid silos? In her research, Dr. Barbakoff has found no evidence that any one structure is inherently better than any other. Both ways have potential advantages and disadvantages.

For positions not dedicated specifically to community engagement, participants reported that community-led programming had to compete with other responsibilities that were built into their job descriptions and into the library's service model. As one person in a generalist position put it, "Capacity is an issue in terms of . . . still [having] traditional reference responsibilities and other internal tasks. So, I think that becomes the pull between . . . [having] to staff the desk to a certain extent and keep the library running, unless you have a different model." Participants also noted that generalists accepted their current jobs not necessarily understanding or expecting to do community-led work, so adoption was uneven.

On the other hand, participants who were in specialized roles related to community engagement or EDISJ often reported feeling isolated. They sometimes felt unable to get others in the organization to understand and engage with their work, even when their responsibilities or relationships overlapped. There were also questions of how people moved into community-engagement roles in the first place. Some participants observed staff being reassigned into outreach roles without much regard for the person's aptitude or interest, or even as a way of disempowering staff viewed as disruptive.

Structural considerations are still vital, even though no specific structure was a magic bullet. Instead, what mattered was whether a person's role included sufficient autonomy and authority (see step 10), and the extent to which community-led work was infused throughout the organization.

In the context of this step, autonomy and authority are not just about managing time, but also about having freedom from rigid roles, procedures, and busywork that cause communication silos and dampen connections. The spirit of the structure should be "designed to support rather than contain" and allow everyone access to opportunities to lead. One librarian imagined a world where "the structure of one's organization ideally would be based on freedom, openness, fewer assigned tasks, and more shared goals." Participants wanted the freedom to determine how to have a meaningful impact.

Structurally, participants emphasized how important it is to decentralize and democratize participation in community-led work, regardless of what role someone holds. Their libraries flourished when they fostered a culture that understood and embraced a community-led perspective from every position. As one participant expressed this idea in their journal: "For me, the most important takeaway from the conversation was [that] the holistic organizational approach is the way to scale this work to the rest of the system."

Strategies for Success: Engaging Staff in All Positions

Making community-led planning the work of all staff does not have to mean major changes like rewriting job descriptions and reorganizing departments (although it certainly can!). In the context of your library's size and structure, consider how staff can contribute and engage from within the scope of their jobs. For example, one key thing leaders can do is write support and expectations for all staff to engage in community-led work into their strategic plans and annual goals. This encourages budget, staff time, and other resources at all levels to be directed toward community-led training and activities. Those who do directly manage community-led planning processes should take time to share their knowledge, experience, and perspective with others on staff, including those who do not conduct the same kind of work. For example, they may present at a staff meeting or share regular email updates.

Libraries can also take steps to engage staff in any position or type of work, including those who do not engage directly in planning. All staff can be encouraged and supported in accessing at least some training on community-led concepts, as described in step 2. All staff can be encouraged to try new things in the scope of the work to support community, and have any failures embraced as a learning milestone. All staff can have their identities validated and celebrated, and their perspectives and contributions treated as valuable. All staff can be given opportunities to share their ideas for new programs, services, or partners based on their own lived experiences.

Addressing Pitfalls: Shifting Mindsets

In many ways, this step is a test of the inspirational and transformational changes you have made so far. You are now asking people in many roles to do something different or new in their jobs. Has the culture shifted enough to bring people along? If not, you may encounter resistance from staff. This can be a sign that more needs to be done to help shift people's mindsets.

Community-led work fundamentally shifts the power dynamic between the library and the community.[2] It challenges traditional perceptions of the library's identity and role. The resulting changes may run counter to staff ideas of what their job is or should be. Staff may feel intimidated by seeing work shift away from clear procedures and defined expectations to ambiguous situations with limited control over the process and results. (For more on addressing this, refer back to step 5, on developing psychological safety.) But deeper resistance can come from discomfort with the way community-led work may challenge people's professional identity and their idea of what a library looks like.

In a community-led model, the library is no longer the place with all the answers. Important knowledge comes from outside, implicit in the community. Our worldview shifts from a needs-based to an assets-based perspective, which again centers expertise and therefore power in the community, rather than in the library. We are forced to reckon with systems of oppression that exist in our libraries. We are called to change our practices, moving away from the safety of pushing out our knowledge and resources to the far more vulnerable position of leading with questions.

These are deeply challenging shifts. That is why we cannot simply skip to the operational phase of change—adjusting budgets and schedules, creating positions, reassigning work, rewriting performance evaluation criteria, etc.—without doing deep cultural work to shift mindsets first. Even after all you have done, there will be some resistance. However, if that resistance is widespread, persistent, and severe, this may be a sign that you need to back up and reinvest in shifting culture and mindsets.

 CASE STUDY · McCracken County Public Library

Location	Racial demographics	Staff size
Paducah, Kentucky (population 65,397)	87% White, 11% Black, 1% Hispanic or Latine, 1% Other	37.5 on staff: 32 librarians, 6.25 with MLIS degrees

Located in western Kentucky, the city of Paducah anchors a mostly rural region located near the confluence of the Mississippi and Ohio Rivers. The McCracken County Public Library is also a confluence of different people and organizations.

This story shows how the library made community-led librarianship everyone's work by embracing an all-hands-on-deck approach that got staff out of the building and excited about the potential of working with the community in new ways.

When Susan Baier moved to Paducah from Los Angeles, California, in January 2017 to become the library's director, many in the community saw the library very traditionally, as a place for books and lectures and storytimes, and little more.

Even though the library had already been working with community partners, Baier made it her mission to raise the library's profile as a community partner. She did so by trying to get both herself and her library staff out into the community more.

While most community coalitions are eager for members and volunteers, they often don't think of the librarians as members of their coalitions. Librarians in turn may feel out of place showing up in a new environment, like party crashers.

Mike Muscarella met Baier through a third-party organization, the local Rotary Club. Muscarella has led the community coalition Healthy Paducah since it started in 2014. He gave a presentation to the Rotary on their health park initiative, and afterward Baier approached him and said she and the library wanted to be involved in their coalition.

This meeting initiated a layering of community outreach. First, Baier joined the Rotary, then through the Rotary she joined Healthy Paducah. That connection positioned the library to become involved in a health fair, host flu shots, and transform the local perception of public libraries as health partners.

Muscarella said Baier embodies the ideals of a personal touch combined with a goal of connecting the entire community to the library. He described how active and visible she is in the community, saying, "she not only gets information about what's going on in our community, she lives it."

A visionary library director can only go so far. To truly transform communities, the entire library has to be engaged and excited. It has to become everyone's work.

McCracken County only has one public library location, and so reaching the whole population requires leaving the building. Baier decided that the library had to find a way to have a presence at every single school's Back to School Festival. With a dozen McCracken County Public Schools locations, this was not a trivial matter. But Baier and her staff made it work, embracing the ethos of "all hands on deck." Everyone went out, including Susan herself, to ensure that every single student and family in the county knew about the library and its resources.

Youth services manager, Linda Bartley, also embraced this ethos with her staff, taking library staff to schools and after-school settings so that connections can be formed across the institution, and not just with library administrators.

The library's community partners, such as the local United Way, have also adopted the idea that more can be accomplished for the community when multiple organizations contribute their own unique strengths. Anne Bidwell of the United Way says that the library is perhaps the strongest nonprofit in all of McCracken County, in part because of working alongside and with the community to address concerns.

Bidwell said that through her work with the United Way, she developed a close working relationship with the school's coordinator for transitional (i.e., homeless) youth. With Paducah's winter temperatures averaging in the 30s, staying warm is a critical need. A partnership between the schools and United Way ensures these students have the clothing they need for the winter months. When the school had some winter coats leftover, Bidwell connected the school to the library.

The United Way, the school, and the library then worked together to figure out how to distribute the coats. Because there was no day shelter for the homeless in Paducah, the library is that shelter. Many agencies that serve the low-income population require documentation that cannot be produced by those who are homeless, but the library, with no stipulations, has built trusting relationships within the homeless community. "None make you feel safe, like the library can and does," said Bidwell. So it made sense for these three partners to join forces to get coats to those in need.

The success of this project was possible because of the outreach and engagement Baier and her staff had cultivated with the many community partners striving to improve health and wellness in McCracken County. "I did not know half the stuff that Susan was doing with our homeless population until we brought that committee together. And she shared and that was just mind blowing. So it really opened up my eyes to just how important our library is. And the reach it has," said Muscarella.

The library started weaving itself into the community by empowering library staff to integrate their passions into their librarianship and inviting the community to become engaged. Emerging organically over thirty years, these layers were reinforced by a library director who prioritized joining committees and getting involved in multi sector projects, like Healthy Paducah. Library administration worked alongside staff and provided them with the resources to be successful as they were encouraged to get outside of their comfort zone.

TAKEAWAYS

1. Making community-led librarianship everyone's work may require a combination of both carrots and sticks: hard requirements (like everyone has to take on a back-to-school shift) and soft encouragement (use who you know to get started) proved to be successful in Paducah.
2. Find ways to connect the work you do off-site to the work you do in your library. Simple things like always signing up people for library cards can connect the pieces together and make it easier to justify and sustain.

Summary of Step 11

Libraries have the greatest capacity for community-led work when everyone in the organization has some level of training on and responsibility for it. Many different structures can support this infusion. What matters most is that the structure is designed to encourage open communication rather than silos; maximize staff autonomy in how work gets done; and authentically value the lived experiences, perspectives, and contributions of all staff. Regardless of whether or not your library has specialized positions, it should support all staff with the opportunity and flexibility to engage with the scope of their jobs. Be aware that these operational changes to job activities, even when small, can challenge deep-seated beliefs about the identity of libraries and librarians. Some resistance is expected, but if changes are failing to take hold, it may be a sign that you need to return to a previous phase and invest more in transforming culture and mindsets.

NOTES

1. Jeff Dyer, Hal Gregersen, and Clayton M. Christensen, *The Innovator's DNA: Mastering the Five Skills of Disruptive Innovators* (Harvard Business Review Press, 2011).
2. John Pateman and Ken Williment, *Developing Community-Led Public Libraries: Evidence from the UK and Canada* (Ashgate Publishing, 2013); Working Together Project, *Community-Led Libraries Toolkit* (2008), www.vpl.ca/sites/default/files/Community-Led-Libraries -Toolkit.pdf.

Measure Success through Relationships

What It Means

We may start out with community-led work because we believe it is important, a way to put our EDISJ goals into action as part of our communities. But what keeps us going? How do we persist and sustain community-led work when it gets hard? The question of sustainability is the root of this final step.

Meta-analyses of motivation research have resulted in the theory that effectance (also called effectiveness, efficacy, or agency) is the root human motivation that drives most action.[1] In short, we keep doing things when we think we are doing a good job of making a difference on something that matters. When we have no yardstick to validate our impact or progress, our motivation suffers—and so does the sustainability of our approach. This is a challenge for community-led work because its impact is not easily measured by traditional library statistics.

Libraries tend to rely on some common output measures to track success. These include door counts, circulation counts, number of reference questions, number of programs, and program attendance. By these measurements, community-led programs may not appear highly successful, at least at first. For example, community-led programs are generally slow to develop (meaning fewer of them take place) and may be designed to serve a highly specific population (meaning potentially fewer attendees). Over time, a strong community-led approach may lead to larger, more diverse groups of patrons coming through the doors, checking out materials, or attending programs. But as this is a cumulative effect and many other factors can influence usage metrics, it would be difficult to later trace these changes back to a single cause.

At the same time, traditional outputs do not effectively measure the things that community-led planning is designed to achieve. This is in part because outputs measure something related to the *product*, but the real value of community-led work is the *process*. One of the key indicators of the success of a community-led initiative is the strength of the relationships it has built, especially with BIPOC and excluded communities. Another is how much impact it had on an issue or goal that the community has identified as important. These are outcomes and impacts, not outputs. They are often easy to feel but hard to measure. This makes them difficult to communicate to an outside stakeholder who was not there—say, a director, a board member, a potential funder, or the local newspaper.

Measuring what matters helps make community-led work more sustainable. Being able to document and communicate success is motivating to staff and compelling to organizational leaders, potential supporters and partners, and community members. Libraries should adjust the metrics they collect to focus on two areas: the process of relationship building and the impact on community-chosen goals.

Focusing on relationship building as a process is important because many relationships do not turn into concrete initiatives, yet the work of building authentic relationships free from predetermined expectations of deliverables is highly valuable and essential. Relationships are required for community-led initiatives to begin, and they are also a result of working together closely.

To understand the impact on community goals, the library should help identify the community's definition of success at the start of a community-led process. This means working together to understand what impacts the community cares about most, deciding how progress toward those goals will be measured or observed, and making a plan for collecting and sharing supporting data.

To measure relationships and impact on community goals, libraries may need to expand their evaluation toolbox. For example, they may need to utilize qualitative methods more effectively, beyond surveys—such as by training staff on observation techniques and conducting follow-up interviews. They may also rethink what numerical data they collect. For example, they might collect quantitative indicators related to the process of building relationships, such as number of community meetings attended, number of partners, what percentage of partners or participants in a specific initiative are from the intended community of focus, or how many partners return for multiple engagements. Whatever is measured or documented, the library should collect this type of information in a centralized and standardized way, much as it likely does with output metrics, so that it becomes a regular part of the way staff think about success.

Exploring the Evidence

Librarians who continue to invest in community-led planning think about success differently. They believe that the relationship, not the concrete deliverable, is the real result that matters. To them, the process *is* the product. For example, how many people came to a program was far less important to them than how well the planning process deepened a relationship with a community that the library had previously not served well. In one particularly illuminating example, a librarian had offered a program that used a traditional library-led planning method one year and then repeated the same type of event using a community-led model the following year. Using only standard outputs, the two years looked similar: for example, the programs had similar attendance. However, they differed notably in terms of the relationships they built. The librarian described it more fully:

> The success that I defined was that we were able to develop strong relationships with new partners in the community. And now we're good friends and I can call on them for support or information or maybe our paths will converge again, and we can do something else together. And then hopefully, it's more reflective of our community. . . .

> What was really cool was some of our partners who work specifically with people of color, they brought their community. And so what was once . . . typically, I would say, dominated by White, older women, it was a very diverse—there were kids there—it was very diverse looking, more than before. And it was cool, and I knew it wouldn't have happened if we hadn't involved them.

In this example, the success that mattered was connecting with the full spectrum of the community and developing meaningful, ongoing relationships.

However, community-led librarians often felt frustration by the mismatch between what they could measure and what mattered to them. They felt they had few methods for demonstrating success during a community-led process, compared to a tangible deliverable like a program or report. They needed ways to show internal stakeholders that the investment in time was worth it. One participant summed it up by saying, "People believe in the value of relationships and trust and community connection, but we don't know how to articulate that or speak to that well enough in libraries, period."

Participants struggled to communicate their impact to leadership. Librarians in the study believed that communicating success to leaders was an essential strategy to increase organizational support for their work, yet none said they were doing this effectively. Some felt pressured to produce a high volume of less meaningful programs or services in order to report "good" numbers. Individuals tried a variety of strategies like creating infographics, collecting testimonials, or writing wrap-up or annual reports. When asked about their most important takeaways or single most desired change, multiple participants focused on "develop[ing] ways to better demonstrate the value of relationships and collaboration with community."

Strategies for Success: Develop a Theory of Change

Theory of Change, sometimes called logic modeling or outcomes-based planning, is one potential strategy for aligning what you measure with the impacts you want to have. This method surfaces and clarifies our assumptions about how change will take place. It allows us to identify a cascade of small, measurable steps that would logically lead to the large-scale, hard-to-measure impacts we hope to have.

A Theory of Change model consists of a few key elements. Most notably, it is a backward planning model. Instead of beginning with the project you want to undertake, you begin with the big-picture change you hope individuals or communities will experience. This may be something you cannot measure. Then you work backward to determine a smaller or shorter-term change that would likely lead to the larger change. For the smaller change, identify an indicator—something you can measure or observe to help you know if progress is taking place. You may do this several times, until you have indicators you can readily collect. That's what you'll measure. From there, you can plan your service by considering what actions will move the needle on your indicator(s) and what resources are needed to support those actions.

In a community-led process, of course the community itself will define what the goals and steps are, with the library providing support or facilitation for the process of articulating them. You will work with the community to develop your Theory of Change before the planning process begins, not at the end. It is essential not to assume that everyone sees success in the same way, or finds the same kinds of measurements or indicators meaningful, as this may differ significantly between cultures, people, and situations. Assumptions are often rooted in bias and lead to misunderstandings. If not surfaced early, they can derail the entire process as each partner is working for different ends. By defining collectively what success looks like and how you will evaluate it from the very start, you can have clear, informed dialogue about what actions will be most effective and meaningful.

Theory of Change is a common tool in the nonprofit sector and has been adapted to a library specific context by such resources as *Five Steps of Outcome-Based Planning and Evaluation for Public Libraries* by Gross, Mediavilla, and Walter and the Research Institute for Public Libraries (RIPL), a project of the Colorado State Library and Colorado Library Consortium.[2] The brief outline provided here provides a short introduction to concepts more thoroughly explored in such resources.

Addressing Pitfalls: Making Your Own Tool

Libraries will likely need to make their own tools and procedures to collect and house the data they decide to collect. This can be a challenge, especially in libraries with limited staffing. No current, widely adopted library-specific tool exists for this purpose. Major industry-wide tools for understanding and measuring success tend to focus on outputs, with a few venturing into predetermined outcomes under a specific set of circumstances. Even if such a tool did exist, it could not cover every eventuality because communities will develop their own definitions and indicators of success for individual projects. Therefore, to measure success as it relates to relationship building with partners over time, libraries will need to find, adapt, or develop tools for themselves.

Devising ways to define and collect your data does not need to be too daunting. You can use sophisticated tools and systems if you have access to and funding for them, or you can stay as simple as a spreadsheet. The important thing is to integrate your new types of data into your existing systems and processes. Try not to silo them into a separate place or timeline. For example, if staff fill out a monthly spreadsheet of statistics, update your template to include the new metrics, and link to the written Theory of Change that explains why they matter. Collect longer-form information like surveys, comment cards, and reports in a central place, review them on a regular basis, and communicate summaries of what you learn to all staff. Because community-led planning is a different way of looking at your current work, and not an additional layer of new work, it should be integrated into your everyday processes as seamlessly as possible.

CASE STUDY · Belgrade Community Library

Location	Racial demographics	Staff size
Belgrade, Montana (population 12,960)	93.5% White, 2% Native American, 2% Hispanic or Latine, 2% Other	7 on staff: 7 librarians, 2 with MLIS degrees

In 2015, the Belgrade Community Library received *Library Journal*'s coveted Best Small Library in America award. According to library director Gale Bacon, central to the library's success has been its promotion of positive relationships both internally and externally.

As a hands-on library director, Bacon makes a point of taking a shift at the library's circulation desk at least once a week. Bacon also has a paperwork structure in place to document programs and partnerships— binders of information that staff can turn to if someone is unavailable or leaves the library.

As a result of this documentation system, when the former children's services librarian left the library and Benjamin Elliott joined the staff, he was able to immediately make connections with the library's partners, ensuring that the relationships endure across the staff transition.

Elliott also said that one of the first things Bacon did when he joined the library was enroll him in a community development course offered through the local chamber of commerce. Elliott said the course helped him get to know all about the town quickly, including meeting people from sectors as diverse as agriculture, transportation, education, and law enforcement.

Elliott said that his ability to form relationships so quickly with a variety of community partners enabled him when he developed library programs— he did so in a way attuned to other happenings in the community. For example, Elliott reached out to a local nonprofit focused on youth and worked with them to compare their schedules so that they wouldn't inadvertently be competing for their audience's time, and they could instead work together on youth programming.

Similarly, Lisa Beedy of the Belgrade Senior Center said that she appreciates—due to the strong relationship she has with the library—being able to let the library take certain programming areas. The senior center doesn't need to be all things to all people, and neither does the library, because they're working together rather than apart.

The library also measures success through documentation of its community relationships. Adult services librarian Sarah Creech has such a strong relationship with Beedy of the Belgrade Senior Center that when Beedy got sick with COVID-19, Creech was the very first person Beedy reached out to.

TAKEAWAYS

1. Develop staff onboarding mechanisms to enable new staff to come up to speed quickly with existing community relationships.
2. If you're in a position of administration, work hard to keep relationships going, and stay attuned both to internal and external dynamics.

Summary of Step 12

The final step in building your library's capacity for community-led planning focuses on making your changes sustainable. To continue motivating staff engagement, leadership support, and community buy-in, align what you measure with what really matters. Elevate process over product by focusing your definition of success on the strength and diversity of your relationships rather than the outputs of your projects. Collaborate with your community to identify what success means to them, and then decide collectively how it looks and how to measure it. By making relationship-based, process-focused, community-defined data a normal part of your evaluation processes, you can encourage sustainable, ongoing investment in community-led planning.

NOTES

1. Richard E. Clark and Fred Estes, *Turning Research into Results: A Guide to Selecting the Right Performance Solutions* (Information Age Publishing, 2008).
2. See Melissa Gross, Cindy Mediavilla, and Virginia A. Walter, *Five Steps of Outcome-Based Planning and Evaluation for Public Libraries* (ALA Editions, 2016).

PART

V

Evaluating, Adapting, and Troubleshooting

Just like community-led initiatives themselves, the internal process of growing your organization's capacity to engage in them is complex and dynamic. To apply the framework in this book to your unique and evolving environment, you will need to evaluate and adapt along the way. This chapter focuses on how to conduct evaluation of your CoLaB process formally or informally, and what to do when you spot a problem.

The CoLaB framework is not intended to be linear. Although it is presented in discrete, ordered steps for clarity, in practice the steps may overlap, loop, be skipped, or even be used individually. This is because each library will begin with a different level of capacity and its own unique set of strengths and challenges. In some areas, you may already feel you have reached your goal. For particularly challenging areas, you may find yourself returning to a single step or set of steps again and again. If you have very limited capacity or support, you might focus on just one step before even considering any others. Additionally, as you follow the steps in this book, your community and your library will continue to shift. A significant event in the community or a change in leadership at the library could prompt you to jump ahead or return to a previous stage. This framework is a garden. It is meant for you to get out your tools, dig in, and make it your own.

Evaluation Questions

For each of the twelve steps, we provide a question you can use at multiple points throughout your process to help understand where you are starting and what kind of progress you are making. These questions can be used formally or informally. For example, if you are undertaking a formal change management process based in the CoLaB model, the project manager could ask these questions as part of a focus group at the start and end of each phase. If a small group is working together informally on just a few steps, you could meet to have conversations about these questions throughout the process. Or if you are working mostly alone, you could periodically set aside time to journal your own responses to these questions. No matter how formal or informal, there are a few key moments where you may find it particularly helpful to ask evaluation questions and make changes.

At the Beginning and End of Each Step and Phase

Good evaluation starts at the beginning of planning, not at the end. Reflecting on the evaluative question before beginning the work helps you understand where you are starting from. Exploring and articulating your initial context helps you predict how challenging the step is likely to be, so you can allot the right amount of time or resources. It may prompt you to think about who needs to be involved in this phase for it to be most successful. Asking a question before you begin a step can also help you determine if this really is the right next step for you, or if it should be adapted, skipped, or delayed.

The questions you asked in the beginning are also essential to helping you evaluate at the end. Having a pre- and postmodel gives you a baseline for comparison that enriches your understanding of what happened. This is particularly important for culture work, which is difficult to measure. We quickly get used to how things are now, blurring our perception of where we started and making it hard to see how far we have come. When you ask yourself the same question at the end, compare it to your initial responses. Consider if you have improved or changed, how much, and in what ways. Is it enough to move your focus to the next step, or is there more work to do first? Under what circumstances might you want to revisit some or all of this step?

During a Step

There are two points during a step where returning to the evaluation question can be especially helpful. These are as part of a regular evaluation process, or at a point of difficulty. If you are conducting a formal change process in your organization, then you should have regular evaluation built into your plan. Include the evaluative questions in team meetings, or return to them on a set timeline (for example, once a month) to gauge progress. This can be helpful in identifying issues or successes early, as well as in restoring focus and generating new ideas. Even if you are making changes informally or alone, it may be illuminating to plan to ask yourself the evaluative questions on a regular basis.

When you encounter a challenge, one of the first things you can do is turn to the evaluative question for that step. Consider why your answer has changed from the beginning, or why the needle seems stuck. What has changed or what you have learned that perhaps you did not expect at the start? Evaluative questions can help shed light onto what may be going awry, and prompt creative conversations or reflections on solutions.

The questions associated with each step are listed in the tables below.

Phase One: Inspirational Change

Step	Evaluative questions
1. Set clear expectations and accountability for EDISJ.	How important would you say EDISJ and community-led work are to your organization's leadership? How would you rank their commitment on a scale of 1 to 10? Why did you choose that number?

(continued on next page)

Phase One: Inspirational Change (*cont'd*)

Step	Evaluative questions
2. Educate for understanding instead of training for procedure.	How would you now describe the connection between community-led programming and equity, diversity, and inclusion? Thinking of the professional development that you have pursued or that the library has provided lately, how has that changed or informed your understanding of the connection?
3. Connect to core values and community goals.	How important do you think community-led methods are for supporting our community and increasing equity, diversity, and inclusion? Say, on a scale of 1 to 10? Why did you choose that number?
	Try to articulate how community-led work connects to the library's core values or an important community goal. How easy or difficult was that to do? Why?

Phase Two: Transformational Change

Step	Evaluative questions
4. Foster a growth mindset.	How confident do you feel in your own ability, or in the ability of your team collectively, to learn and improve at community-led planning? Say, on a scale of 1 to 10? What, if anything, do you think would make you feel more confident?
5. Develop psychological safety to support a culture of inclusive innovation.	To what extent do you feel that all staff are safe to share disruptive ideas and engage in open communication? Say, on a scale of 1 to 10? Why?
	To what extent do you think our library supports a culture of innovation and inclusion related to community-led work? Say, on a scale of 1 to 10? Where are we doing well, and where could we improve?
6. Make time and space for reflection.	To what extent have you engaged in reflective processes related to community-led programming? What did you learn? What kinds of support and time do you receive for reflecting, and how helpful have they been?
7. Prioritize interpersonal skills and cultural humility.	How highly would you rate your own interpersonal (or "soft") skills, especially when interacting with people whose cultural identity and lived experience differ significantly from yours? Say, on a scale of 1 to 10? How about the skills of your team? How effective has the library been in helping you develop these skills?

Phase Two: Transformational Change (*cont'd*)

Step	Evaluative questions
8. Apply prior knowledge.	Describe how some of your prior experiences, including in other jobs or outside of work, have helped you feel prepared to be successful with community-led programming. What skills and knowledge do you bring that you hadn't realized?
9. Build community knowledge through relationships.	Describe steps you have taken to learn about your community recently. What have you learned about your community? In what ways did you engage with community partners to gain this knowledge, if at all? Have you engaged in any structured inquiry, like asset mapping or community assessment? How about informal learning?

Phase Three: Operational Change

Step	Evaluative questions
10. Give staff time, flexibility, and autonomy to build relationships.	In general, do you have the amount of time you need to spend building community relationships? Would you say you have too little time, too much time, or the right amount? What could be changed to improve this? When building community relationships, have you had the autonomy you needed to be flexible with your community-led goals, activities, and schedule? Would you say you have not enough decision-making power, too much, or the right amount? What could be changed to improve this?
11. Make it everyone's work.	To what extent would you say that staff across the organization are supported in participating in community-led work? Say, on a scale of 1 to 10? How does the structure of your organization support or limit your ability to engage in community-led work? How might you work across divisions or hierarchies to engage more people or parts of the library?
12. Measure success through relationships.	How does your library measure the success of a program, service, initiative, or change now? What statistics or feedback do you regularly collect and use? Who decides what to count or measure, and who decides what counts as success? How easy or difficult is it to connect your measurements to impact on community goals?

When Things Go Awry

What can you do when a step does not seem to be working? You may be encountering resistance, or maybe change just doesn't seem to take hold no matter what you try. First, check that you did not overlook or rush the phase of transformational change. Jumping to operational changes too quickly, before the change makes sense in the culture, can cause people to ignore or reject the new procedure. Culture-shifting work takes time and relationships—mirroring the community-led work it supports—and so progress may take more time than expected.

Next, return to the chapter describing the step where you are stuck. What are the fundamental concepts and principles behind what you are trying to accomplish? Why is this step important to the work and to your library? Returning to the big ideas can help you imagine new ways to achieve them, rather than focusing too narrowly on how to tweak your existing solution. Check the "Addressing Pitfalls" section to see if a solution there might help.

If none of these remedies are enough, it is time for some deeper analysis of why you are facing an issue. Sometimes, an issue persists because our solutions are addressing the wrong problem, or only part of the problem. Especially in complex organizations like libraries, it is easy to hold an inaccurate or overly simplistic assumption about what is causing the issue. Understanding the root cause is critical.

There are many tools available to help with root-cause analysis. One of the simplest is called "5 Whys." This method is commonly used as part of Six Sigma. All it entails is asking "Why is this happening?" five times in a chain. The purpose of the 5 Whys is to understand the deeper causes motivating a surface issue. For example:

I asked my manager for more time to reflect (step 6), but they keep asking me to do other tasks anytime they see me sitting quietly at my desk. They just don't support me or care about community-led work!

Wait, why is that happening? (1)
    a. Because they think I'm not doing anything.

Why is that happening? (2)
    b. Because it looks like I'm just sitting there.

Why is that happening? (3)
    c. There's no way for them to know that I'm reflecting quietly rather than just wasting time.

Why is that happening? (4)
    d. Because I haven't indicated on my calendar or in my space that I've blocked that time out to reflect.

Why is that happening? (5)
    e. I guess I didn't think I needed to do that! But now I realize that I do. Maybe it's not that they don't support my request—maybe they just didn't realize they were interrupting my reflection time.

In this example, the asker starts with a problem—having their reflections interrupted—and an assumption about the manager's motives. By the end of the 5 Whys, they have identified the real issue and challenged their assumption. After identifying the root cause, the next step is to identify an action you can take to address it. In this example, the person might put out a "Do not disturb" sign, create a calendar invitation for their manager, or go to a different part of the building during reflection time.

5 Whys is just one type of root-cause analysis. If you cannot settle on a likely root cause or causes, or if your solutions repeatedly fail, you may want to try a different option. For a particularly thorny issue, you may benefit from a more complex tool like causal-layer analysis (developed in the strategic foresight field), potentially with an outside facilitator or trained staff member. Regardless of the tool used, keep in mind that the purpose is to identify the underlying causes of a problem. Then try out solutions that address the real issue, rather than putting a bandage on its surface manifestation.

Summary

This twelve-step model is intended to be used in a nonlinear way. Evaluation is essential to determining how to adapt the model to make it work best for you. Evaluation should be baked in from the beginning of your change process and embedded throughout and not something you do only at the end; this is so you can learn and adapt as you go. In this chapter, we've included question prompts for each step to support your evaluation work, however formal or informal it may be. Because every library, community, and point in time is unique, it is expected that you will encounter some challenges or a need for change. If you feel stuck even after returning to the relevant chapter, try a root-cause analysis tool like the 5 Whys to understand and respond to the underlying issue. Evaluating your own work is not so different from the reflection you do as part of your community-led planning, so you have already been building this muscle.

CONCLUSION
Moving Forward and Coming Back

C ongratulations! By working your way through the big and small changes described in this book, you have moved your entire library into a deeper, more equitable relationship with the community. Whether you are a senior leader organizing a formal, large-scale change effort with all twelve steps, or an individual trying to influence your organization in whatever ways you can, you make a difference.

In the first section of this book, you learned about the importance of community-led work, its underlying principles, and its basic steps. Then the real work began as you learned to increase your organization's capacity for community-led planning, so that the ideas and steps you learned about could become a sustainable new way forward. Through the twelve steps of the CoLaB model from Dr. Barbakoff and applied case studies from Dr. Lenstra, you began transforming your organization to keep community at the center of all your work. Instead of doing more, you learned to do your current work differently—to focus on process over product, to value relationships over deliverables, and to proactively share power with impacted communities instead of reacting to the loudest voices. Finally, you considered how to conduct evaluation to understand your progress and keep your library accountable. At each step of the way, your library and your community became a tiny bit more equitable, inclusive, and welcoming to all.

As you move forward, remember that communities and relationships are always evolving. Happily, this means a community-led librarian's work is never complete. There is always more to learn about our communities. We have more relationships to build and those to nurture, new goals to strive for, and new ideas to explore together. Keep coming back to this book to help keep yourself, and your library, rooted in what really matters. When we truly share power, the library is the heart of the community, and the community is the heart of the library.

BIBLIOGRAPHY

Ambrose, Susan A., Michael W. Bridges, Michele DiPietro, Marsha C. Lovett, and Marie K. Norman. *How Learning Works.* Jossey-Bass, 2010.

American Library Association. *American Library Association Strategic Directions*. 2017. www.ala.org/aboutala/sites/ala.org.aboutala/files/content/governance/StrategicPlan/Strategic%20Directions%202017_Update.pdf.

———. *Diversity Counts!* 2007. www.ala.org/aboutala/sites/ ala.org.aboutala/files/content/diversity/diversitycounts/diversitycounts _rev0.pdf.

———. *Equity, Diversity, Inclusion: An Interpretation of the Library Bill of Rights*. 2017. www.ala.org/advocacy/intfreedom/librarybill/interpretations/EDI.

Asset-Based Community Development Institute. "Values behind ABCD." DePaul University, n.d. https://resources.depaul.edu/abcd -institute/about/Pages/Values.aspx.

Bandura, Albert. "Exercise of Human Agency through Collective Efficacy." *Current Directions in Psychological Science* 9, no. 3 (2000): 75–78. https://doi.org/10.1111/1467-8721.00064.

———. "On the Functional Properties of Perceived Self-Efficacy Revisited." *Journal of Management* 38, no. 1 (2012): 9–44. https://doi .org/10.1177/0149206311410606.

Barbakoff, Audrey. "Building Capacity for Equity, Diversity, and Inclusion in Public Library Programs through Community-Led Practices: An Innovation Model." PhD diss., University of Southern California, 2021.

Berk, Josh. "Mental Health Training in Public Libraries." *Public Libraries*, January 5, 2015. http://publiclibrariesonline.org/2015/01/mental-health-training-in-public-libraries/.

Bertrand, Marianne, and Sendhil Mullainathan. "Are Emily and Greg More Employable than Lakisha and Jamal? A Field Experiment on Labor Market Discrimination." *American Economic Review* 94, no. 4 (September 2004): 991–1013.

Blackburn, Fiona. "Community Engagement, Cultural Competence and Two Australian Public Libraries and Indigenous Communities." *IFLA Journal* 43, no. 3 (2017): 288–301. https://doi.org/10.1177/0340035217696320.

Bryson, J., and B. Usherwood. *Social Impact Audit.* South West Museums Libraries and Archives Council, 2002.

Burke, W. W. *Organizational Change: Theory and Practice.* Sage, 2018.

Burke, W. Warner, and George H. Litwin, "A Causal Model of Organizational Performance and Change." *Journal of Management* 18, no. 3 (1992): 523–45. https://doi.org/10.1177/014920639201800306.

Caspe, M., and M. Lopez. "Preparing the Next Generation of Librarians for Family and Community Engagement." *Journal of Education for Library and Information Science* 59, no. 4 (2018): 157–78. https://doi.org/10.3138/jelis.59.4.2018-0021.

Cecchi-Dimeglio, Paola. "How Gender Bias Corrupts Performance Reviews, and What to Do About It." *Harvard Business Review*, April 2017. https://hbr.org/2017/04/how-gender-bias-corrupts-performance-reviews-and-what-to-do-about-it.

Chi, M. T. H., M. Bassok, M. W. Lewis, P. Reimann, and R. Glaser. "Self-Explanations: How Students Study and Use Examples in Learning to Solve Problems." *Cognitive Science* 13 (1989): 145–82. https://doi.org/10.1207/s15516709cog1302_1.

Clark, Richard E., and Fred Estes. *Turning Research into Results: A Guide to Selecting the Right Performance Solutions.* Information Age Publishing, 2008.

Coghlan, David, and Mary Brydon-Miller, eds. *SAGE Encyclopedia of Action Research.* SAGE, 2014.

Community Foundation of Anne Arundel County. *Poverty Amidst Plenty VI: On the Road to Progress for All, 2018*, 6th ed. 2019. www.aacounty.org/boards-and-commissions/partnership-for-children-youth-families/forms-and-publications/2018-needs-assessment-poverty.pdf.

Cooke, Nicole A. *Information Services to Diverse Population: Developing Culturally Competent Library Professionals.* Libraries Unlimited, 2017.

———. "The Spectrum Doctoral Fellowship Program: Enhancing the LIS Professoriate." *InterActions: UCLA Journal of Education and Information Studies* 10, no. 1 (2014). https://doi.org/10.5070/D4101018980.

Dweck, Carol S. *Mindset: The New Psychology of Success.* Ballantine Books, 2008.

Dweck, Carol S., and Daniel C. Molden. "Mindsets: Their Impact on Competence Motivation and Acquisition." In *Handbook of Competence and Motivation: Theory and Application*, 2nd ed., ed. A. Elliot, C. Dweck, and D. S. Yeager, 135–54. Guilford Press, 2018.

Dyer, Jeff, Hal Gregersen, and Clayton M. Christensen. *The Innovator's DNA: Mastering the Five Skills of Disruptive Innovators.* Harvard Business Review Press, 2011.

Eccles, J., and A. Wigfield. "In the Mind of the Actor: The Structure of Adolescents' Achievement Task Values and Expectancy-Related Beliefs." *Personality and Social Psychology Bulletin* 21 (1995): 215–25. https://doi.org/10.1177/0146167295213003.

Edmondson, Amy C. *The Fearless Organization: Creating Psychological Safety in the Workplace for Learning Innovation and Growth.* John Wiley & Sons, 2019.

———. "Psychological Safety and Learning Behavior in Work Teams." *Administrative Science Quarterly* 44, no. 2 (1999): 350–83. https://doi.org/10.2307/2666999.

Edmonton Public Library. *EPL Community-Led Toolkit.* 2016. https://epl.bibliocms.com/wp-content/uploads/sites/18/2015/08/EPL-Community-Led-Toolkit-Final-EXTERNAL-Web.pdf.

Elliot, A. J., and C. S. Hulleman. "Achievement Goals." In *Handbook of Competence and Motivation: Theory and Application*, 2nd ed., ed. A. J. Elliot, C. Dweck, and D. S. Yeager, 43–60. Guilford Press, 2018.

Ewenstein, Boris, Wesley Smith, and Ashvin Sologar. "Changing Change Management." McKinsey, July 1, 2015. www.mckinsey.com/featured-insights/leadership/changing-change-management.

Garmer, Amy K. *Rising to the Challenge: Re-envisioning Public Libraries.* Aspen Institute, 2014.

González, Rosa. *The Spectrum of Community Engagement to Owner-ship: Facilitating Power*. Facilitating Power, 2020. www.facilitating power.com/spectrum_of_community_engagement_to_ownership.

Gross, Melissa, Cindy Mediavilla, and Virginia A. Walter. *Five Steps of Outcome-Based Planning and Evaluation for Public Libraries*. American Library Association, 2016.

Hart, Roger A. *Children's Participation: From Tokenism to Citizenship*. UNICEF, 1992. www.unicef-irc.org/publications/pdf/childrens _participation.pdf.

Harwood Institute for Public Innovation. *A Step-by-Step Guide to "Turning Outward" to Your Community*. 2015. www.ala.org/tools/ librariestransform/libraries-transforming-communities/resources -for-library-professionals.

Hentschke, G. C., and P. Wohlstetter. "Cracking the Code of Account-ability." *Urban Education*, Spring/Summer 2004, 17–19.

High Point Public Library. "Sensory Garden." n.d. www.highpointnc .gov/2563/Sensory-Garden.

Horrigan, John B. "Libraries 2016." Pew Research Center, September 9, 2016. www.pewinternet.org/2016/09/09/2016/Libraries-2016/.

Huff-Eibl, R., J. F. Voyles, and M. M. Brewer. "Competency-Based Hiring, Job Description, and Performance Goals: The Value of an Integrated System." *Journal of Library Administration* 51, nos. 7–8 (2011): 673–91. https://doi.org/10.1080/01930826.2011.601270.

IAP2 Spectrum by the International Association for Public Participa-tion, n.d. Available at https://iap2usa.org/cvs.

IDEO. *Design Thinking for Libraries: A Toolkit for Patron-Centered Design*. 2015. http://designthinkingforlibraries.com.

Institute of Museum and Library Services. *Transforming Communities: Institute of Museum and Library Services Strategic Plan, 2018–2022*. 2018. www.imls.gov/ sites/default/files//publications/documents/ imls-strategic-plan-2018-2022.pdf.

International Association for Public Participation. *The Spectrum of Public Participation*. n.d. www.iap2.org/page/pillars.

Jaeger, Paul, and Renee Franklin. "The Virtuous Circle: Increasing Diversity in LIS Faculties to Create More Inclusive Library Services and Outreach." *Education Libraries* 30, no. 1 (2007): 20–26. https:// doi.org/10.26443/el.v30i1.233.

Kania, John, Mark Kramer, and Peter Senge. *The Water of Systems Change*. FSG, 2018. http://efc.issuelab.org/resources/30855/30855.pdf.

Kemmis, Stephen, Robin McTaggart, and Rhona Nixon. *The Action Research Planner: Doing Critical Participatory Action Research*. Springer, 2016.

Kim, Kyung-Sun, and Sei-Ching Joanna Sin. "Recruiting and Retaining Students of Color in LIS Programs: Perspectives of Library and Information Professionals." *Journal of Education for Library and Information Science* 47, no. 2 (2006): 81–95. https://doi.org/10.2307/40324324.

Klinenberg, Eric. *Palaces for the People: How Social Infrastructure Can Help Fight Inequality, Polarization, and the Decline of Civic Life*. Crown, 2018.

Koontz, Christie, and Barbara Gubbin. *IFLA Public Library Service Guidelines*. De Gruyter Saur, 2010. https://doi.org/10.1515/9783110232271.

Krathwohl, David R. "A Revision of Bloom's Taxonomy: An Overview." *Theory into Practice* 41, no. 4 (2002): 212–18. https://doi.org/10.1207/s15430421tip4104_2.

Kretzmann, John, and John McKnight. *Building Communities from the Inside Out: A Path toward Finding and Mobilizing a Community's Assets*. Center for Urban Affairs and Policy Research, Northwestern University, 1993.

Lashley, Eric P. "The Level of Community Engagement in Texas Libraries." *Texas Library Journal* 93, no. 3 (2017): 78–79.

Lenstra, Noah, and Martha McGehee. "How Public Health Partners Perceive Public Librarians in 18 US Communities." *Journal of Library Outreach and Engagement* 2, no. 1 (2022): 66–80.

Mestre, L. "Librarians Working with Diverse Populations: What Impact Does Cultural Competency Training Have on Their Efforts?" *Journal of Academic Librarianship* 36, no. 6, (2010): 479–88. https://doi.org/10.1016/j.acalib.2010.08.003.

Monroe, Margaret E. "Community Development as a Mode of Community Analysis." *Library Trends* 24, no. 3 (1976): 497–514.

Muddiman, Dave, Shiraz Durrani, John Pateman, Martin Dutch, Rebecca Linley, and John Vincent. "Open to All? The Public Library and Social Exclusion: Executive Summary." *New Library World* 102, no. 4/5 (2001): 154–58. https://doi.org/10.1108/03074800110390626.

Northouse, P. *Leadership: Theory and Practice*. 8th ed. Sage, 2018.

Pateman, John, and Ken Williment. *Developing Community-Led Public Libraries: Evidence from the UK and Canada*. Ashgate Publishing Company, 2013.

Pew Research Center. "From Distant Admirers to Library Lovers: A Typology of Public Library Engagement in America." April 13, 2014. http://libraries.pewinternet.org/2014/03/13/typology/.

Rath, Tom, and Barry Conchie. *Strengths Based Leadership: Great Leaders, Teams, and Why People Follow*. Gallup Press, 2008.

Reid, H., and V. Howard. "Connecting with Community: The Importance of Community Engagement in Rural Public Library Systems." *Public Library Quarterly* 35, no. 3 (2016): 188–202. https://doi.org/10.1080/01616846.2016.1210443.

Sonnie, Amy. *Advancing Racial Equity in Public Libraries: Case Studies from the Field*. Government Alliance on Race and Equity, 2018. www.racialequityalliance.org/wp-content/uploads/2018/04/GARE_LibrariesReport_v8_DigitalScroll_WithHyperlinks.pdf.

Surette, S. "The Challenge of Evaluating Community-Led Work." *Feliciter* 59, no. 5 (2013): 13–15.

Tench, Beck. "Designing Restoration: Protecting and Restoring Our Attention through Participatory Design." PhD diss., University of Washington, 2022.

———. *The Library Workers' Field Guide to Designing & Discovering Restorative Environments*. 2022. restorativelibrary.org.

Thompson, L. L., and C. Fuller-Gregory. *The Movement toward Equity*. Public Libraries, 2020. http://publiclibrariesonline.org/2020/05/the-movement-toward-equity/.

Totten, Herman L. "Ethnic Diversity in Library Schools: Completing the Education Cycle." *Texas Library Journal* 76, no. 1 (2000): 16–19.

University of Kansas Center for Community Health and Development. *Community Tool Box*. 2020. https://ctb.ku.edu/en.

University of North Carolina at Greensboro, School of Education. "HEAL (Healthy Eating and Active Living) at the Library." Let's Move in Libraries, n.d. https://letsmovelibraries.org/about-us/heal/.

Vinopal, Jennifer. "The Quest for Diversity in Library Staffing: From Awareness to Action." In the Library with the Lead Pipe, 2015. www.inthelibrarywiththeleadpipe.org/2016/quest-for-diversity/.

Wigfield, Allan, Emily Q. Rosenzweig, and Jacquelynne S. Eccles. "Achievement Values: Interactions, Interventions, and Future Directions." In *Handbook of Competence and Motivation: Theory and Application*, 2nd ed., ed. Andrew J. Elliot, Carol S. Dweck, and David S. Yeager, 116–34. Guilford Press, 2017.

Working Together Project. *Community-Led Libraries Toolkit.* 2008. www.vpl.ca/sites/default/files/Community-Led-Libraries-Toolkit.pdf.

INDEX